Older workers:
the view of Dutch employers in a European perspective

OLDER WORKERS:

the view of Dutch employers in a
European perspective

Wieteke Conen

netherlands
interdisciplinairy
demographic
institute

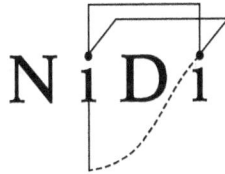

N i D i

Book 88

Koninklijke Nederlandse Akademie van Wetenschappen

Routledge
Taylor & Francis Group

LONDON AND NEW YORK

First published in 2013 by Amsterdam University Press Ltd.

Published 2025 by Routledge
4 Park Square, Milton Park, Abingdon, Oxon OX14 4RN
605 Third Avenue, New York, NY 10158

*Routledge is an imprint of the Taylor & Francis Group,
an informa business*

ISBN: 9789069846651 (pbk)
ISBN: 9781003700814 (ebk)
ISSN 0922-7210

For Product Safety Concerns and Information please contact our EU
representative: GPSR@taylorandfrancis.com
Taylor & Francis Verlag GmbH, Kaufingerstraße 24, 80331 München,
Germany

Table of contents

1. Organisations dealing with an ageing workforce: views and behaviour across time and place

1.1. Introduction

Since the mid-1990s, European governments have been using various sets of policy instruments to achieve extension of working lives and cope with the consequences of an ageing population. In a labour market context, active ageing refers to continuing participation in the labour force, 'giving older people the chance to participate fully in society' and 'promoting job opportunities for older people' (European Commission, 2012). But even though policymakers at the country level may agree on and be convinced of the necessity to extend working lives, whether this macro-goal can and will actually be achieved depends on individual workers' and employers' behaviour. Acknowledging the role of different stakeholders in the process of active ageing, this study seeks to provide more insight into whether employers' behaviour has been changing over time and how European employers are behaving towards older workers.

It is important to study employers' behaviour towards older workers for a number of reasons: scientific reasons, reasons related to issues at the macro level of society, reasons related to organisational policy-making and reasons related to consequences of employers' behaviour for older workers. First of all, this study addresses several research questions regarding employers' attitudes and behaviour towards older workers that have received limited attention in the scientific literature to date. One gap this study addresses is that although we know that governments have been changing the institutional surroundings in order to prolong working lives, there is only limited insight into whether employers have been changing their attitudes and behaviour towards working longer over time. This study enhances our knowledge 'whether' and 'how' employers make the transition from early withdrawals to prolongation of working lives. A second void this study aims to fill is the extent to which employers support the extension of working lives from an internationally comparative perspective. To that aim, unique data on employers' attitudes and behaviour towards older workers has been collected.

Furthermore, from a macro-level perspective, the combination of an ageing population and early withdrawal from the labour force has substantial consequences for welfare state expenditures. Therefore, according to governments and experts, nations and labour markets are in need of higher participation rates of older workers. Knowledge of employers' attitudes and actions towards older workers and their views on prolongation of working lives makes it easier to anticipate the feasibility of policy measures in this field. But also on a meso-level, organisations may benefit from knowledge of employers' policies and practices towards older workers when developing and introducing personnel policies.

A final reason for this study can be found in the consequences employers' behaviour has on older people's possibilities to (re-)enter or stay on the labour market. In the near future, many older workers may want to, or financially need to, work longer, but whether workers will be able to continue working will also largely depend on the willingness of employers to continue employing them. Knowledge of employers' recruitment and retention behaviour and implemented personnel policies gives more insight into the extent and type of organisations that are supporting —or not supporting— prolongation of working lives.

This study was carried out within the framework of a research project called 'ASPA', which is an acronym for 'Activating Senior Potential in Ageing Europe'[1]. This project was initiated as a joint effort by Utrecht University and Netherlands Interdisciplinary Demographic Institute and was funded as part of the EU 7th Framework research programme under the Socio-economic Sciences and Humanities theme (2008-2011). Participating research institutes in the project are from Denmark, France, Germany, Italy, the Netherlands, Poland, Sweden and the United Kingdom. The project aimed at examining the forces and mechanisms behind employers', civil society organisations' and governments' behaviour towards older people

[1] This research was funded by the EU Framework Programme Seven (FP7/2007-2013) under grant FP7-216289 (ASPA). I gratefully acknowledge all consortium members for data collection and suggestions: Per Jensen from Aalborg Universitet (Denmark), Annemarie Guillemard, Marielle Poussou-Plesse and Denis Duplan from Ecole des Hautes Etudes en Sciences Sociales, CEMS/IMM (France), Frerich Frerichs and Paula Aleksandrowicz from the Research Centre for Ageing and Society (CAS) at the University of Vechta (Germany), Giovanni Lamura, Andrea Principi and Carlos Chiatti from the Department of Gerontological Research of the Italian National Research Centre on Ageing (INRCA) (Italy), Kène Henkens and Harry van Dalen from the Netherlands Interdisciplinary Demographic Institute, KNAW/NIDI (Netherlands), Joop Schippers from Utrecht University (Netherlands), Jolanta Perek-Bialas and Konrad Turek from Jagiellonian University, Krakow (Poland), Dominique Anxo from Centre for Labour Market Policy Research, Linnaeus University (Sweden) and Robert Lindley and Beate Baldauf from Warwick University (UK). See for more information: http://www.aspa-eu.com/

and the resulting societal arrangements. In this book, the *employers'* views and practices towards older workers are central. Within the ASPA-project, international survey data was jointly collected with all consortium partners on the topic of employers' attitudes and behaviour towards older workers. Furthermore, all consortium partners conducted case study research at the organisational level in their own country. Both the international survey data and Dutch case study research are used in this book.

This study on employers' attitudes and behaviour towards older workers should be seen against the background of demographic trends, as well as developments in labour market participation and changes in policy contexts in Europe. This background will be described in section 1.2. In section 1.3, I will elaborate on related previous research and the new research questions this study addresses. Next, in section 1.4, I will discuss some theoretical considerations concerning employers' behaviour towards older workers. The data will be discussed in section 1.5 and at the end of this introductory chapter I will present a brief overview of the outline of this book and formulate the central research questions.

1.2. Ageing and the labour market in Europe

1.2.1.   Demographic developments
In the coming years, European countries will face an unprecedented transformation due to the ageing of the population. Although population ageing affects all regions of the world, it is most advanced in Europe (Van Nimwegen and Van der Erf, 2010). *Figure 1.1* and *figure 1.2* present the demographic parameters which underlie the onset of an ageing population and workforce; *i.e.* the total fertility rate and life expectancy at birth, respectively. In this chapter, I will present figures on countries involved in the ASPA project: Denmark, France, Germany, Italy, the Netherlands, Poland, Sweden and the United Kingdom. Where possible, I will include an EU average.

Figure 1.1 shows that the total fertility rate of European countries changed considerably during the 20th century. The figure starts in the early sixties, when Poland and the Netherlands had a relatively high fertility rate with more than three children per woman, whereas Sweden, Germany and Italy had a fertility rate near replacement level. With the commercial introduction of the pill as contraception method, fertility rates dropped sharply. The overall impression of fertility levels in European countries is that all countries went

Figure 1.1. Total fertility rate (1960-2010) and projected total fertility rate
(2015-2060) in the ASPA countries, mean number of children per woman

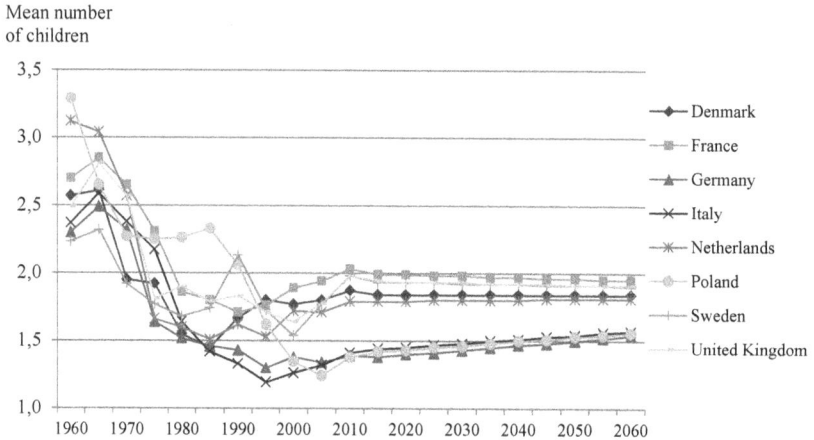

Sources: [a] Statistics for the period 1960-2010 are retrieved from Eurostat's
Demography database (2012);
[b] Projections for the period 2015-2060 are retrieved from EUROPOP2010
(2012). More about methodology at http://epp.eurostat.ec.europa.eu/
[c] Eventual missing figures for the period 1960-1985 are inserted from
United Nations Statistics Division (2012).

from a state of high fertility to a state below replacement levels – although
the pace and timing of the decline differs across countries. The *communis
opinio* among Eurostat forecasters seems to be that around 2060 fertility
rates converge around the level of 1.71 for the EU as a whole (European
Commission, 2011a); in all EU countries fertility rates are expected to stay
below the natural replacement rate in the period to 2060.

Figure 1.2 portrays the development in life expectancy of men and women
in Europe. One observation to be made is that life expectancy differed
considerably between countries in the sixties, but life expectancy at birth
converged during subsequent years. Second, whereas in 2010 life expectancy
of Northern, Western and Southern countries converged to a relatively high
level, Poland (and also other Eastern European countries) still lag behind.
Life expectancy is expected to increase further for the next fifty years and
around 2060 male life expectancy in Europe is projected to be 84.6 years,
while female life expectancy is projected to be 89.1 years (European
Commission, 2011a).

Figure 1.2. Life expectancy at birth (1960-2010) and projected life expectancy at birth (2015-2060) in the ASPA countries, males and females, mean number of years to be lived at birth

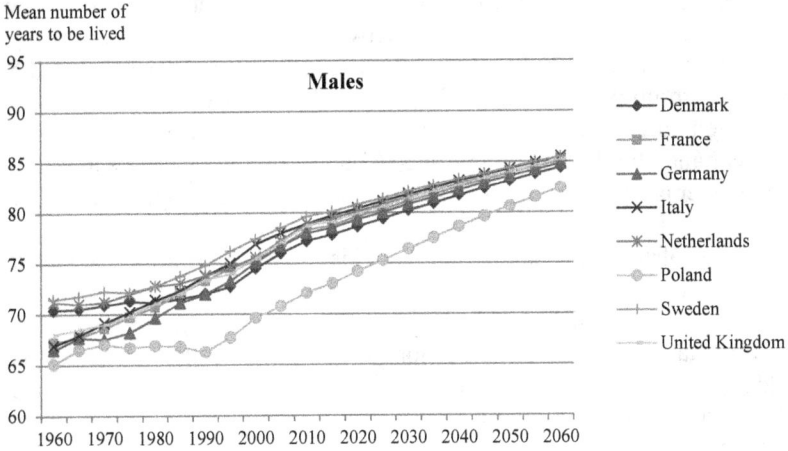

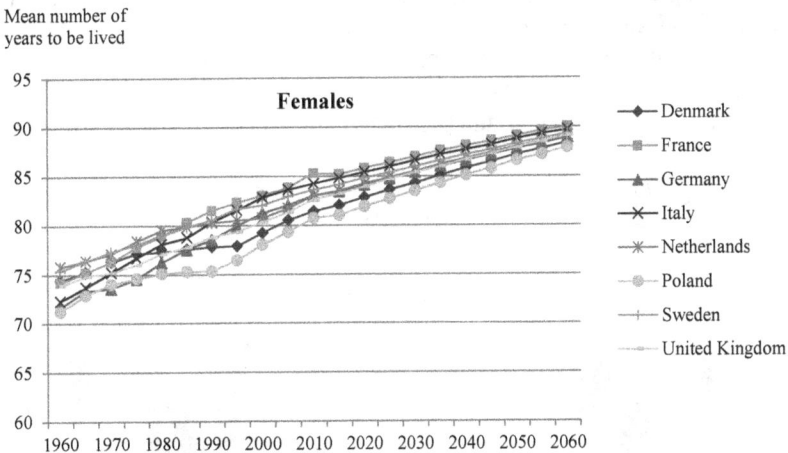

Sources: [a] Statistics for the period 1960-2010 are retrieved from Eurostat's Demography database (2012);
[b] Projections for the period 2015-2060 are retrieved from EUROPOP2010 (2012). More about methodology at http://epp.eurostat.ec.europa.eu/
[c] Eventual missing figures for the period 1960-1985 are inserted from United Nations Statistics Division (2012).

The demographic developments described above have significant consequences for the population structure in Europe. In all countries, the share of people aged 15 to 64 —*i.e.* the share of the population from which employers usually recruit their staff— will decline over the next decades. Whereas the average share of people between 15 and 64 constitutes 67 per cent on average in 2010, this will have decreased to around 57 per cent in 2050. *Within* the group of people aged 15-64, the share of workers in the second part of their career will increase, having major effects for organisations. On the other hand, the share of people aged 65 and older will increase in Europe: from on average 17 per cent in 2010 to 29 per cent in 2050 (Eurostat, 2012).

The process of an ageing population is not identical in all European countries. The main reason for this is the moment fertility rates have started to decline and the speed at which the fertility rate changed. As *figure 1.3* shows, Germany, Italy and Spain will be among the countries with the highest share of older people in 2050, while the United Kingdom and the Nordic countries will have a relatively young population. But also for these relatively 'young' countries the share of persons of 65 years of age and older will have almost doubled during the first half of this century.

These demographic developments have significant consequences for the number of old aged and the (potential) workforce over time. The old age dependency ratio is an age-population ratio of those typically not in the labour force (dependent) and those typically in the labour force (productive) and measures the pressure on the productive population. *Figure 1.4* presents

Figure 1.3. Percentage of population aged 65 years and over in Europe, 2010-2050

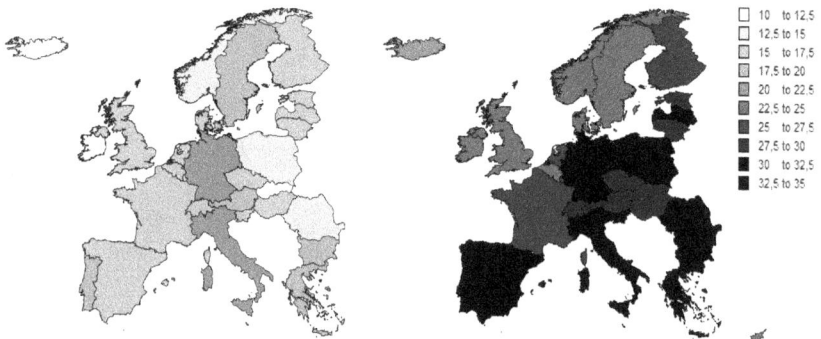

Source: Eurostat, 2012.

*Figure 1.4. Old age dependency ratio (1960-2010) and projected old age
dependency ratio (2015-2060) in the ASPA countries, ratio of the persons aged
65 and more over the number of persons of working age (15-64)*

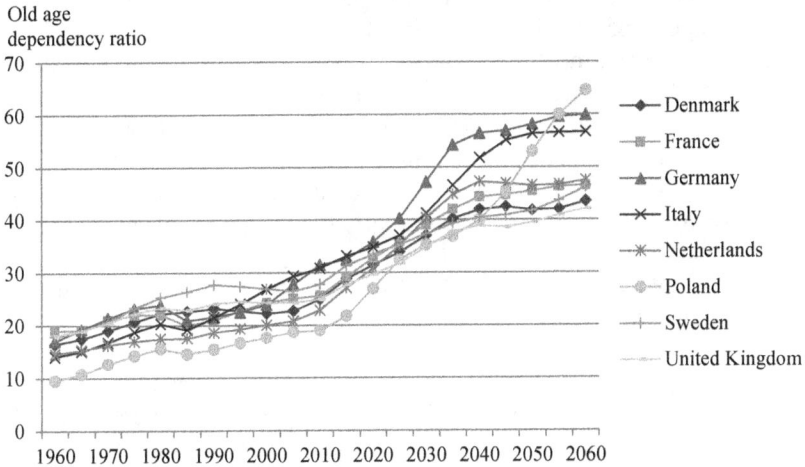

Sources: [a] Statistics for the period 1960-2010 are retrieved from Eurostat's
Demography database (2012);

[b] Projections for the period 2015-2060 are retrieved from EUROPOP2010
(2012). More about methodology at http://epp.eurostat.ec.europa.eu/

[c] Eventual missing figures for the period 1960-1985 are inserted from
United Nations Statistics Division (2012).

the ratio of the population aged 65 years or over (dependent) to the population
aged 15 to 64 (productive) in all relevant countries.

In the sixties, Poland had the lowest old age dependency ratio (9.5 persons
aged 65[+] per 100 persons of working age) and France the highest (19 persons
per 100). Until 2010 the figure shows a gradual increase in the old age
dependency ratio, but the consequences of the ageing population will be felt
particularly in the coming decades as the potential labour force decreases
and the number of pensioners increases. In 2010 the number of old aged
as a percentage of the potential labour force in Europe is approximately 25
per cent, in other words: every pensioner is potentially supported by four
workers. The old age dependency ratio will increase steeply in the coming
decades as in 2060 every pensioner will probably be supported by two
workers. This old age dependency ratio increases dramatically in Poland,
Germany and Italy, and to a lesser extent in the United Kingdom, Denmark
and Sweden.

1.2.2.   Changing contexts
The demographic developments as outlined in the previous section will have major consequences for the welfare state. In countries with an official retirement age of 65, the first post-war babies reached the age of 65 in 2010. In the coming years, most members of the populous baby-boom generation will leave the labour market. An increasing number of seniors will depend on old-age pensions, and more people depending on care will lead to rising health care costs. Furthermore, the share of people that contribute in terms of taxes and social security premiums is falling. Enlarging the pool of productive workers, including raising participation levels of older workers and extending people's working life, is seen by both experts and policy makers as a key element in facing the consequences of an ageing population and the rising welfare state expenditures.

The demographic developments will also have large consequences for the labour market. The emphasis in the labour market will increasingly be transferred towards older workers, as younger cohorts of men and women will constitute a smaller share of the working population. Furthermore, although in the short run the current economic crisis enlarges labour pools, the ageing of the population is expected to have a negative effect on the effective labour supply in the long run (*cf.* European Central Bank, 2008). Predictions are that younger cohorts may not suffice to replace the large number of retirees (*i.e.* labour shortages will arise), unless age and sex specific participation rates will increase, or in a future scenario in which the demand for labour decreases. In that light, raising the participation levels of underrepresented groups —amongst which older workers— came to be regarded as an important instrument to deal with expected demographically-induced labour shortages.

The 1994 EU Summit was the first to underline the need to improve employment opportunities for older workers. In March 2001 the European Council of Stockholm defined, for the first time, a quantitative and highly ambitious target in this respect —in addition to the overarching strategic goals set at the Lisbon European Council in 2000— by determining that by the year 2010 the employment rate of older workers should rise to 50 per cent (from 26.3% in 2000) (European Council, 2001). At the Barcelona European Council it was clearly stated that responsibility for tackling issues arising from an ageing population will need to be shared between the generations: "A progressive increase of about five years in the effective average age at which people stop working in the European Union should be sought by 2010" (European Council, 2002, p. 12).

Later, the EU-Commission assessed the progress achieved towards the Stockholm and Barcelona targets in its communication on *'Increasing employment of older workers and delaying the exit from the labour market'* and has judged it to be insufficient (European Commission, 2004). The Member States were asked to take drastic action and develop comprehensive active ageing strategies. This requirement has been endorsed by the report of the Employment Taskforce (Employment Taskforce, 2003) which emphasised that a radical shift in policy measures, away from a culture of early retirement, was necessary and that the challenge was not only to ensure a higher share of those currently aged 55 to 64 stayed in work, but also to enhance the employability of those aged in their 40s and 50s. The EU committed itself to supporting this development through policy co-ordination, the exchange of experience and of best practices and through financial instruments (European Commission, 2004). The EU Green Paper on demographic change (European Commission, 2005) once again underlined the nature of the challenge Europe is facing and the urgency to take action.

The *Common actions for growth and employment* report (European Commission, 2005) promotes 'active ageing', which is seen as contributing to the overall objective of the European Commission of improving people's living standards. In its communication entitled *"The demographic future of Europe – from challenge to opportunity"* (European Commission, 2006) the European Commission again highlights the importance of improving work opportunities for older people and increasing potentially productivity and competitiveness by valuing the contributions of both younger and older employees. This initiative does not aim at adopting a new plan, but rather to ask member states to systematically integrate ageing population in all policies, and to reinforce their actions in this direction.

Between 2006 and 2011, the work of the Commission to stimulate increasing labour force participation of older workers continued. The European Commission organised a *European Forum on Demography* in 2006, 2008 and 2010 and installed a special expert group on demographic issues, with "the main task of assisting and advising the Commission in the development of policies geared to the Union's new demographic reality, as well as monitoring population and workforce developments in terms of ageing" (Commission Decision 2007/397/EC). The Commission's *Renewed Social Agenda* identified population ageing as one of the key drivers of societal change in Europe (European Commission, 2008a) and under the theme of *Meeting Social Needs in an Ageing Society, the Demography Report 2008* appeared (European Commission, 2008b), providing an up to date inventory of needs and opportunities of an ageing population. The report *Employment and Social Developments in Europe 2011* (European Commission, 2011b) contains an extensive chapter on active ageing and employment of older workers. Finally, the Commission declared 2012 the *European Year for Active Ageing and Solidarity between Generations.* According to the website, the year is 'intended to raise awareness of the contribution that older people make to society and to encourage policymakers and relevant stakeholders at all levels to take action with the aim of creating better opportunities for active ageing and strengthening solidarity between generations'.

Of the year 2012, in many individual member states early exit has been rethought. In the majority of (old) member states, *e.g.* in Austria, Belgium, Denmark, Finland, France, Germany, Italy, the Netherlands, the United Kingdom and Sweden, there have been pension reforms to curtail or to restrict access to early exit schemes and programmes. The motivations for these changes were cost containment and financial balance in the face of an ageing population (see OECD, 2000). This motivation may lead to national policies promoting an increase in the number of working years, without necessarily implementing a systematic approach to cope with the consequences for the actors involved.

The average effective age of retirement visualises changes in retirement behaviour. As shown in *figure 1.5*, between the early 1970s and the mid-1990s, there was a clear trend for male and female workers to withdraw earlier and earlier from the labour market. Early retirement was incited by both a massive use of early exit routes, such as early retirement schemes, disability pensions and unemployment benefits, and —in some countries— by the lowering of standard pension ages. Increases in the effective retirement age since the mid-1990s have only partially reversed these falls. From a historical perspective, *extension* of working lives is a relatively new phenomenon.

Over the last decade, labour force participation of older workers has increased and workers have been gradually extending their working lives (Eurostat, 2012). Rising participation rates of older workers are often ascribed to a mixture of factors, such as changed institutional contexts inciting older workers to extend working lives, higher educational attainment by later cohorts of older workers, an increase in female labour force participation (partly via women's increased investment in education), and an increase of non-standard employment contracts among older workers (such as self-employment, temporary employment and part-time employment). Nevertheless, not all member states met the Lisbon target set by the 2001

Figure 1.5. Average effective age of retirement by gender in the ASPA countries, 1970-2007

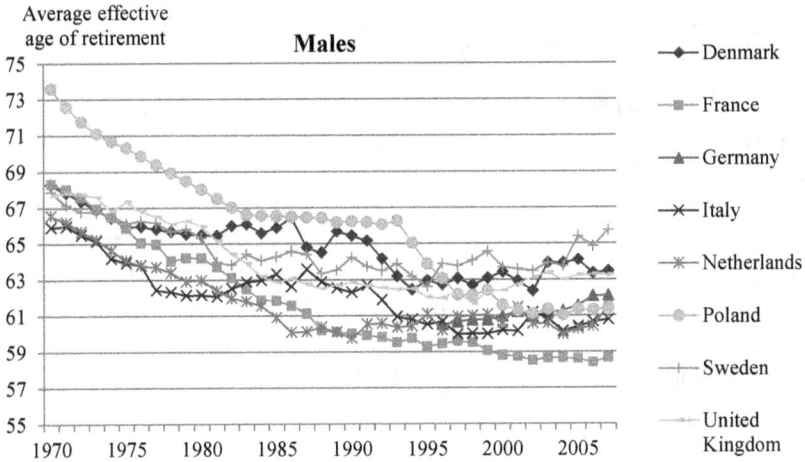

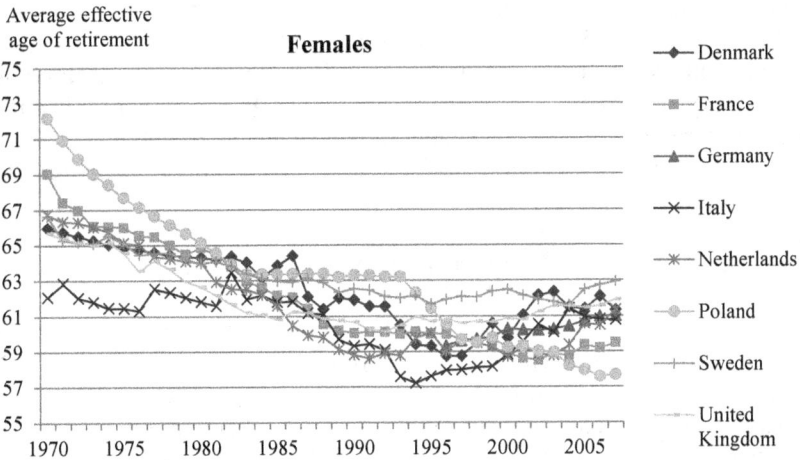

Source: OECD, 2011.

Table 1.1. Employment rate by age groups and gender in the ASPA countries, 2011 (percentage)

Geopolitical entity	50-54 years		55-59 years		60-64 years		65-74 years	
	Male	Female	Male	Female	Male	Female	Male	Female
EU27	*81.9*	*69.6*	*70.3*	*55.2*	*39.0*	*24.5*	*10.5*	*5.8*
Denmark	83.6	80.0	78.1	74.8	49.6	36.2	14.8	6.6
France	85.3	75.4	67.4	60.5	20.4	17.4	4.5	2.8
Germany	86.4	77.5	80.1	67.7	52.2	36.3	9.4	5.0
Italy	85.4	56.4	67.4	43.8	29.5	12.8	8.7	2.5
Netherlands	86.8	73.1	82.2	61.9	49.2	30.8	12.1	5.2
Poland	73.3	66.4	62.0	39.1	30.3	13.5	10.7	5.0
Sweden	88.3	85.5	83.7	80.3	68.1	58.2	15.6	7.9
United Kingdom	83.0	77.0	74.1	65.8	54.6	34.1	17.5	11.2

Source: Eurostat, 2012.

Stockholm Council, targeting at a 50 per cent employment rate of older workers by 2010. Furthermore, despite these upward sloping participation trends, in most countries employment rates still drop considerably for workers between 55-59 years and drop sharply after the age of 60 (see *table 1.1*). In addition, the mean and median age of retirement is often well below the statutory age of retirement (Eurostat, 2012). In other words, in most countries early retirement is still rather the rule than the exception. A country such as Sweden is an exception, performing relatively well in retaining older workers for the labour market.

European countries have implemented contrasting policies with different results in relation to the work life extension and increasing labour force participation of older workers. In 2012, Scandinavian countries have the best results regarding retention of older workers on the labour market. Belonging to the category of Social Democratic welfare states, most of these welfare states are large and comprehensive but also very costly. This requires high labour force participation rates (Esping-Andersen, 1990), and hence most segments in the population have been mobilised to participate in the labour market throughout history. Essentially, this always has been a necessary condition to be able to 'afford' this type of welfare state. Although Scandinavian countries are by no means homogenous in their policy approach towards older workers and differ greatly in for instance employment protection and labour market policies, these countries are similar in choosing to reinforce their active labour market policies towards people 45 years of age and older throughout the last decades.

On the other hand, other European countries took a different path. For the sake of saving jobs and fighting (youth) unemployment, many European countries chose to compensate seniors for early withdrawal from the labour market from the end of the 1970s to the mid-1990s. Those countries took a path towards 'early exit cultures' and inactivation of seniors. Since the mid-1990s, their 'challenge' to turn the tide has been much larger than in Scandinavian countries. Some countries, such as the Netherlands and Germany, have managed to put an end to early exit routes and increased their labour force participation of older workers by developing activating employment policies and by welfare reforms. Other countries, such as France, Poland and Italy, have not been able to make impressive changes as yet. *Box 1* gives a short description of relevant public policies in the countries under study. On a general note, over the last decades there has been a stronger focus on policies and programmes stimulating the supply of labour, than on policies and programmes aimed at enhancing the demand for older workers.

1.3.   Research on the labour market for older workers

Research on the labour market participation of older workers has been mainly concentrating on attitudes and behaviour of older workers towards work and retirement, or in other words: on the supply side of the labour market. Against the background of earlier withdrawals from the labour market in most advanced economies since the 1970s, questions on determinants of early exit received increasing attention. A vast area of retirement research flourished and has developed since, studying the impact on retirement behaviour from various disciplines. Economists principally emphasize the impact on retirement behaviour from financial incentives (*e.g.* Blundell *et al.*, 2002; Gruber and Wise, 2002) and non-financial constraints such as health (*e.g.* Bound *et al.*, 1999; Kalwij and Vermeulen, 2008); sociologists mainly consider retirement behaviour to be socially determined by for instance the employing organisation, family life spheres and earlier life experiences in both work and family life (*cf.* Hayward *et al.*, 1998; Henkens, 1998; Raymo *et al.*, 2010, 2011; Damman *et al.*, 2011), and psychologists pay particular attention to psychological processes and commitment that precede the act of retirement (*cf.* Wang and Schultz, 2010).

Box 1   **Public policy background of the ASPA-countries**

SWEDEN – History: Sweden belongs to the family of Social Democratic welfare states, which are typically costly and can best be maintained 'with most people working' (Esping-Andersen, 1990, p. 28). Therefore, throughout history most segments in the population have been mobilised for labour market purposes. Like most European countries, Sweden went through a phase of a shortening of working lives. However, already since the early 1950s the preference for the principle of employment promotion programmes has dominated over benefit options for the unemployed. Although Active Labour Market Policies [ALMP] measures have not explicitly targeted older workers, programmes have had an indirect impact on older workers, for instance by programmes aimed at enhancing prospects of long-term unemployed (Anxo and Ericson, 2011). **Present/Future:** By international comparison, employment rates among senior workers (and women) are high. In Sweden, pensions are interlinked with life expectancy at retirement age. Pensions consist of a guaranteed minimum pension from 65 years onwards, and lifetime earnings which can be drawn between ages 61 and 67. At present, there is a debate in Sweden whether to increase the retirement age to age 75.

DENMARK – History: Denmark also belongs to the Social Democratic welfare states. Within this family, Denmark is often regarded as a liberal outlier and characterized as a golden triangle version of flexicurity. This means a reciprocal and interdependent relationship between three institutional components: (1) low levels of employment protection, (2) generous social security and welfare benefits, (3) an active labour market policy. Denmark has traditionally favoured more passive labour market policies than countries such as Sweden, for instance reflected in generous early retirement benefits and until 2006 older workers did not have full rights to become enrolled in active labour market policy measures. In 2004, the statutory retirement age was lowered from 67 to 65 (Jensen and Madsen, 2011). **Present/Future:** Both female and older workers' employment rates are high in a European perspective, but relatively low compared to other Scandinavian countries. The current debates in Denmark are about raising the retirement age back to 67 again —or even to 71— and then from 2025 onwards to interlink the retirement age with life expectancy.

UNITED KINGDOM – History: The United Kingdom belongs to the Liberal welfare states. From the 1970s to the mid-1990s, labour force participation decreased, though not as much as in many other European countries. Over most of the period since the late 1990s older workers employment rates have been rising; particularly women were causing the increased growth of older labour force participation. The Lisbon target of a 50 per cent employment rate for older workers had been achieved by the year 2000. During the 2000s, both supply side and demand side oriented measures were initiated. Especially the *New Deal 50-plus* placed an emphasis on providing counselling services to help job-seekers into work. Furthermore, the British government sought to make a 'business case' for the greater use of older workers (*e.g.* the *Age Positive* programme promoted qualities of older workers and the value of an age-diverse labour force). Concerns about the sustainability of the public pension system have been the primary driver of government policies. In 2002, a pension commission was establish and a lifting of the retirement age was one of its principal recommendations. **Present/Future:** By international comparison, employment rates among senior workers are high. The retirement age in the United Kingdom used to be 60 years for women and 65 for men, but an equalisation of pension ages to 65 had been set in place in 1995, starting in 2010 and to be completed by 2020. In 2007 the government legislated to raise the retirement age stepwise to age 68 in 2046. UK age discrimination legislation does not prevent employers to mandate retirement at age 65 (Casey and Lindley, 2011).

NETHERLANDS – History: The Netherlands is often regarded a 'hybrid' welfare state, in between Social Democratic and Conservative welfare states (*cf.* Arts and Gelissen, 2002). During the seventies the Dutch developed a strong early exit culture, but at the end of the eighties it was considered to be no longer affordable. The government subsequently closed of the disability route, early retirement and unemployment schemes. Government policies have been mainly targeted on the supply side of the labour market and workers were discouraged to leave the labour market before the official retirement age. In 1995, the participation of all Dutch age groups of older workers was below EU average, but participation rates of older men and women increased considerably since then. The emancipation of women started relatively late, which is particularly felt among older cohorts of women. However, women are catching up with men rapidly. The official retirement age of 65 for both men and women has not been subject to change over the last decades. **Present/Future:** Today, Dutch older workers' employment rates are above EU average. In 2012, the caretaker government accepted the Stability Programme, which states to raise the retirement age stepwise, starting at age 65 in 2013 to 67 in 2024. After this, plans are to interlink the retirement age with life expectancy.

GERMANY – History: The German welfare regime has been characterised as a Conservative-Corporatist welfare state. In Germany, the trend towards early exit started in the early seventies, but became more pronounced in the eighties and early nineties. Also after the reunion of East and West, early retirement was often used to adapt and there was a strong consensus between enterprises, trade unions, the state and workers pro early retirement. Employment rates for older women were particularly low, which is interlinked with the retirement age of 60 for women since 1957. This all resulted in low economic activity rates for older workers. Successive governments have tried to reverse this trend, with policies aimed at reducing age discrimination in the labour market, and closing off early exit routes such as old-age pension for women aged 60 plus, unemployment schemes and reducing disability pensions (Frerichs and Aleksandrowicz, 2011). **Present/Future:** In 2012, male and female employment rates of older workers are above EU average. From 2012 onwards, actuarial deductions apply on withdrawal from the labour market before the age of 65. Furthermore, in 2007 it was decided to raise the retirement age gradually to 67 between 2012 and 2029.

FRANCE – History: Between the 1970s and 2000s, France pursued policies allowing seniors to exit early from the labour force via numerous pre-retirement schemes. Given high unemployment, a 1982 reform lowered the retirement age (with a full pension) from 65 to 60. Especially from the early 2000s, France narrowed early exit pathways such as unemployment schemes (2000) and early exit schemes (2003). The 2003 reform also included a package of measures to change workers' behaviour (such as allowing pensioners to work, phased retirement, disincentives for early retirement) and employers' behaviour (*e.g.* making early exit more expensive). Furthermore, the reform included obligatory collective bargaining on company-level negotiations regarding employment and training for seniors every three years. In 2008, the French government adopted plans to raise the minimum retirement age to 62 (58 years for people doing heavy work), made it possible to extend working lives until the age of 70, and to obtain a full pension French workers have to continue working until 67 instead of 65. In 2009 it became obligatory for firms with at least 50 employees to have an action plan regarding the employment of older employees within a year (on a 1% wage bill penalty), but due to the 'haste' in which such plans were drawn many agreements are considered 'cosmetic agreements' (Guillemard and Jolivet, 2011). **Present/Future:** Nowadays, France has relatively low employment rates for both seniors and juniors. Arrangements to compensate older workers withdrawing from the labour market early have existed for so long, that France formed a solid early exit culture. France has one of the most tolerant pension systems in Europe. In France, there were heavy protests against the changes in the retirement age. In 2012, the new government put back the minimum retirement age for some employees from 62 to 60 years again.

ITALY – History: The Italian system can be classified as a Mediterranean welfare state (Checcucci *et al.*, 2011). Italy has traditionally combined generous pension benefits with scarce active labour market measures addressed to older workers. Employment rates among older workers (especially women) have been relatively low—between the mid-1990s and 2005 even under 30 per cent. During the 1990s, pension reforms were made and the statutory retirement age of 60 for males and 55 for females was progressively increased to 65 and 60 respectively. **Present/Future:** Older workers' participation rates, particularly among women, are still relatively low. Furthermore, demographic projections of the old age dependency ratio are particularly severe for Italy. Whereas under previous governments the debate about raising the retirement age was relatively limp and the retirement age for males was set at 60 years for women and 65 for men, in 2011 the Monti government announced substantial reforms. The new measures enshrine that Italians —both men and women— get to retire at age 66 in 2018.

POLAND – History: Since 2004, Poland is one of the new member states of the European Union. The 1990s and 2000s were marked by major changes in the political, economic and labour market situation. During the 1990s governmental policies were mainly focused on the most urgent problems related to the transition from a socialistic system to democracy and a free market economy. With respect to older people, activation rates of older workers were low and the old pension system in Poland provided huge incentives to retire early. Already in the mid 1990s the need to reform the pension system was evident, which resulted in a serious debate on this topic. In 1999, the old PAYG system was changed into a three-pillar system. After joining the EU in 2004, the shape and goals of public policy making changed. Activation of older generations met some interest of policy-makers, which resulted into *Program 50-plus*, a package of measures directed at increasing the employment of older workers (2004) and was followed by *Solidarity across generations* (2008) (Perek-Bialas and Turek, 2011). **Present/Future:** Currently, employment rates of older generations are among the lowest in Europe. Polish women are eligible for retirement at age 60 and Polish men at age 65. In 2012, the Polish government consented to gradually raise the retirement age to 67; for males this is to be achieved by 2020 and for females by 2040.

Retirement is increasingly considered to be a complex *process* of transitions and adjustments instead of a one-time permanent exit from paid employment. Researchers started examining the 'messy process' of retirement and its blurring boundaries due to for instance retired workers re-entering the labour force and older workers moving into 'bridge jobs' before retiring (Hayward *et al.*, 1994; Wang *et al.*, 2008). Furthermore, whereas retirement research initially tended to frame retirement as a voluntary and employee-driven transition, later studies wondered about the level and determinants of *involuntary* retirement (*cf.* Isaksson and Johansson, 2000; Dorn and Sousa-Poza, 2005; Van Solinge and Henkens, 2007). The influence of early retirement arrangements driving older workers out of the labour market (Dorn and Sousa-Poza, 2005) and perceptions of older workers about the reasons that led to an involuntary early retirement (Henkens *et al.*, 2009) were examined, and *employers* were increasingly recognised as key players in defining opportunities of retirement as well as the opportunities for working longer. Nevertheless, employers' views on the changing nature of retirement are still largely unknown (Wang *et al.*, 2008). In other words, the demand side of the labour market has gained interest in order to examine the opportunities as well as the restrictions employees face in their retirement decisions.

Earlier survey research regarding the demand for older workers has examined employers' attitudes and behaviour towards older workers, addressing questions on stereotypical beliefs about older workers (Guillemard *et al.*, 1996; Taylor and Walker, 1998; Chiu *et al.*, 2001; Henkens, 2005; Eschtruth *et al.*, 2007; Van Dalen *et al.*, 2009a; 2010a), and employment practices towards older workers (Guillemard *et al.*, 1996; Taylor and Walker, 1998; Remery *et al.*, 2003; Henkens *et al.*, 2008; Van Dalen *et al.*, 2010a). A few studies have attempted to make cross-national comparisons, comparing France to the United Kingdom (Guillemard *et al.*, 1996) and comparing Spain, Greece, the United Kingdom and the Netherlands (Van Dalen *et al.*, 2009a; Van Dalen *et al.*, 2010a). These studies addressed questions on opinions, attitudes and to a lesser extent practices towards older workers from an international comparative perspective. Most of these studies on employers' attitudes and behaviour towards older workers based on survey data are mainly descriptive in nature.

A second line of existing research that focused on the demand side of the labour market uses case studies. Case studies in this field often refer to a study of a corporate setting with the intent of getting to a holistic understanding of attitudes or behaviour, using a number of different research methods (such as unstructured interviews, semi-structured interviews, desk research). While survey research may provide insight into the prevalence of organisational attitudes and practices, case study research has been conducted in this area to deal with ambivalent developments and underlying motivations regarding employers' behaviour towards older workers. One area of case study research focuses on identification, drivers and dimensions of good organisational practices in age-conscious personnel policies (Walker and Taylor, 1998; Walker 1999; Taylor, 2006; Frerichs *et al.*, 2012). Other case study research examines the interaction of the retirement process between older workers and the employing organisation (Vickerstaff *et al.*, 2003, Vickerstaff, 2006a; 2006b; Brooke, 2009; Taylor *et al.*, 2010). The results from research on employers' behaviour based on case studies are to be interpreted analytically and cannot be generalised statistically, as this research is based on a few organisations within a specific context; some studies focus specifically on 'best practices' in age-management.

Third, while survey research and case study research provide a picture on a more general level, vignette research offers the possibility to address questions on how managers make decisions regarding older workers on a more individual level (*cf.* Karpinska *et al.*, 2011). In these studies, virtual hiring decisions are made — based on short descriptions of a situation or a person, generated by combining characteristics randomly manipulated by the researcher. This method has the advantage of researcher control over the various levels of independent variables and is suitable to investigate issues that are difficult to examine. On the other hand, vignette experiments are hypothetical by nature and as a result participants may be inclined to act differently than they would have in a real-life situation.

The studies presented in this dissertation are linked to the first two research traditions —survey research and case studies— and will address several research questions regarding employers' attitudes and behaviour towards older workers that have received limited attention in the scientific literature to date. The first issue deals with changes in employers' behaviour in the Netherlands *over time*. So far, little is known about whether employers have been changing their attitudes, behaviour and policies towards older workers in their organisations. I use two approaches to analyse employers' behaviour over time. First, this study examines Dutch employers' recruitment and retention behaviour over time by using survey research. While at the time of the design of the Lisbon targets demographic developments were merely theoretically, employers have started witnessing large cohorts of older workers leaving the labour market in practice. Also a change towards higher shares of workers aged 50 years and older *within* the labour force has become a reality by now. But have employers started stimulating extension of working lives? Have they been recruiting more older workers? And do organisations apply policies to retain older workers? Employers' survey research is used to address these issues. Second, there is not much information on whether changes in institutional surroundings have affected employers' behaviour towards older workers or how business-cycle effects influence their behaviour. To that end, longitudinal case study research among Dutch employers was used.

Second, this study provides an extensive *international-comparative* dimension on attitudes, behaviour and organisational policies towards older workers, offering the opportunity to analyse views and behaviour of Dutch employers in a European perspective. This study uses the first large-scale survey among European employers, in which over 6.000 employers in eight European countries participated (Denmark, France, Germany, Italy, the Netherlands, Poland, Sweden and the United Kingdom), covering all types of European welfare state regimes. On a European level, the extent to which employers support prolongation of working lives and take action to retain older workers is not well documented, a void this study aims to fill. To be more specific, this study examines employers' *behaviour* towards older workers: Do European employers stimulate older workers to continue working until or even beyond the statutory retirement age? Have they been recruiting more older workers? And what policies do organisations have to retain older workers? Furthermore, the study examines employers' *perceptions* on the consequences of an ageing staff with respect to productivity and labour costs and the factors associated with an expected labour cost-productivity gap. Finally, the question on what *governments* can do —according to employers— to increase labour force participation of older workers is addressed in a cross-national perspective. A general issue that has received little attention before is to what extent perceptions and behaviour towards older workers are tied to a specific national context, or whether perceptions and practices are more widely found among employers in Europe.

1.4.   Theoretical considerations concerning employers' behaviour

A basic tenet of organisational theory is that organisations are goal-oriented systems that strive for profit maximization, continuity, and a healthy market position (Kalleberg *et al.*, 1996). Employers' behaviour towards older workers is assumed to be dependent on older workers' contributions in achieving these goals. A microeconomic approach centres on the choices made by firms and reasons that workers are interesting to organisations as long as marginal revenues exceed marginal costs. Institutions enter as setting 'the rules of the game' and constitute restrictions and opportunities for employers' behaviour.

Examining the relationship between age, labour productivity and labour costs often starts from human capital theory (Becker, 1962; for an overview, see Polachek and Siebert, 1993). Human capital theory states that life is made up of two main phases: a first phase in which young people develop their human capital —in terms of knowledge and skills— through education and experience, and a second phase in which they earn income through paid employment. Human capital refers to both formal and informal knowledge obtained, *e.g.* through pre-school learning, education and job-related training. Investments in human capital boost productivity and remuneration of employees is directly related to their productivity. This means an individual's earnings are proportional to his or her human capital stock: the greater one's human capital accumulation, the higher one's earnings. We therefore see that, in principle, people who possess more human capital have a higher income than people with less human capital. Neoclassical theory predicts that the price of labour is in line with labour productivity of the individual worker.

For most people, investments in human capital are largely made during the first two to three decades of their lives. This does not mean, however, that no additional investments are made later in life. Once people have entered the labour market, they acquire new knowledge and skills. Having said that, the supply of human capital and thus the productivity of workers depends not only on positive factors, but also on depreciation. Because knowledge of older technologies becomes obsolete and because people forget, human capital is subject to depreciation.

During the late 1970s, doubts accumulated about the empirical validity of the relationship between age, labour costs and productivity as described by human capital theory (Hutchens, 1989). Lazear (1979) was among the first to address issues such as: Why do jobs exist where wages increase with seniority — regardless of improvements in productivity? His delayed payment contract theory illustrates how employers may have implicit contracts with their employees regarding the relationship between productivity and income over the lifetime: earnings are lower than productivity during the first phase of workers' careers and higher than productivity during the second phase. Such contracts function as an incentive for employees to put enough effort into their work to obtain the higher wages at the end of the implicit contract period. An employee who shirks runs the risk of being fired before the wage premium is obtained. Therefore, delayed compensation works as an incentive for employees to work harder, stay longer with the organisation and transfer human capital to younger generations of workers.

Human capital theory in essence assumes pay and performance to be equal: an employee receives wages according to his or her marginal product. From this theoretical point of view in which equilibria are central, there is no need in examining the demand side of the labour market. Under the assumption of equality between pay and marginal productivity generated by an employee at every point in time, everybody finds his or her place in the labour market. When this equality is no longer a reality, introducing an inequality to the model, not only the supply side of the labour market is relevant, but also investigating the demand side gains significance.

Since labour supply is heterogeneous, employers can never be sure about the productivity of an individual employee. This applies to the existing workforce, but even more so to future staff. Employers are cognizant of their employees' track record within their organisation and they have information about their current productivity. Employers do not know, however, how workers' health will develop as they age, and whether they will be able to keep up with new technological developments. There is even more uncertainty regarding newly recruited employees. Although diplomas, a job interview, references and in some cases a psychological test may provide an idea of the abilities of new personnel, it remains to be seen how productive they will be.

Employers do have access to what Phelps (1972) called 'previous statistical experiences': information on how certain categories of employees tend to behave and develop. Many employers use these statistical experiences to formulate expectations regarding the future productivity of employees who belong to a particular category. Needless to say, the drawback of using averages based on the experiences of groups of employees to formulate expectations with regard to individuals is that no two employees are alike. Having said that, gathering information about the potential productivity of an individual employee can be an expensive exercise, whereas 'statistical discrimination' —selecting staff on the basis of an average group characteristic— is an extremely economic selection method, that is, if the employer's preconceptions and expectations are confirmed.

1.5.   Data collection

1.5.1.   Survey data

This study has been prepared within the project 'Activating Senior Potential in Ageing Europe'. Within the research project, a questionnaire was developed to provide insight into the attitudes and behaviour of employers. This survey took inspiration from earlier survey research in this field. In the early 1990s, Walker and Taylor conducted survey research amongst employers in the United Kingdom, using a questionnaire with an emphasis on stereotypes of and attitudes towards older workers (Taylor and Walker, 1994; 1998). Questionnaires in this line of research —although sometimes conducted among students as the 'next generation managers'— have been used for instance in the United Kingdom (Loretto *et al.*, 2000, Lyon and Pollard, 1997), in the United States (Forte and Hansvick, 1999), New Zealand (Gray and McGregor, 2003; McGregor and Gray, 2002), Hong Kong (Chiu *et al.*, 2001), and Australia (Steinberg *et al.*, 1996). From the 2000s onwards this line of research was further developed particularly in the Netherlands. Questionnaires were complemented by measures on both behaviour towards personnel in general and older workers in particular, personnel policies; norms, and perceived responsibilities of governments, employers and employees. In 2005, the scope was extended to an international survey entitled 'Fair Play for Older Workers', including Spain, the United Kingdom, Greece and the Netherlands. In 2009, within the ASPA-framework, a large-scale comparative survey was developed to study employers' attitudes and behaviour towards older workers in eight European countries: Denmark, France, Germany, Italy, the Netherlands, Poland, Sweden and the United Kingdom (see *figure 1.6*).

This also means that for the first time in this type of research, all types of European welfare state regimes were distinguished. Sweden and Denmark represent Esping-Andersen's (1990) social-democratic welfare state, the United Kingdom stands for the liberal welfare state, the Netherlands, Germany and France stand for the continental/conservative welfare state. As several authors also distinguish a fourth category, the Mediterranean type of welfare state, Italy was also included. Finally, Poland represents the 'new' EU-member states that have accessed the European Union after the break down of the communist regimes from Eastern Europe. The total number of participating organisations amounts to 6,285, employing over 3 million workers in Europe.

Figure 1.6. Participating countries

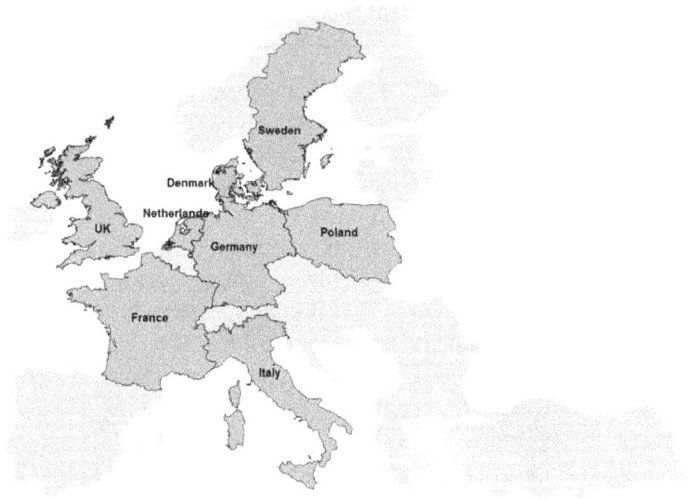

Besides offering the opportunity to make international comparisons, the ASPA-survey also makes it possible to make a comparison to previous rounds of Dutch surveys. To that end, cross-sectional data was pooled from comparative surveys carried out independently among Dutch employers in 2000, 2002, 2005, 2008 and 2009. The questionnaires used in each of the five years contained similar questions on recruitment and retention measures, personnel policies, and features of the organisation.

One of the main objectives underlying the questionnaire was to find out: What are employers' views on older workers in different countries? What do they consider to be the major effects of an ageing workforce? And how can these views be explained? Information was collected on attitudes, behaviours and policies regarding human capital investment during the life course, retirement and recruitment policies, (other) HRM policies, views on the ageing of the workforce and employers' views towards government policies. In general, item nonresponse was rather low; for most questions the response was more than 95 per cent.

Participating research institutes in the ASPA-project carried out the data collection. The total number of completed questionnaires varied per country between N=500 and N=1,087, amounting to a total of N=6,285. Although all national datasets are sizeable, it is difficult to assess to what extent the national samples are representative of the population of interest due to the varying response rates: the overall response rate varies between 7 per cent in France and 53 per cent in Sweden and is 23 per cent on average. These response rates are normal as compared to other corporate surveys: in Europe and the United States response rates in corporate surveys have been found to be at most 20 to 30 per cent (see Brewster *et al.*, 1994; Kalleberg *et al.*, 1996). The variation in response rates may for instance be due to norms among employers to participate in research, varying interview techniques, or due to differences in the organisation of the fieldwork (*e.g.* one versus two reminders sent in Germany and the Netherlands respectively).

A serious problem is that low response rates may give rise to biased results. One reason leading to bias could arise if employers in 'older' organisations would be more inclined to participate in a survey on this topic than organisations with a relatively young staff. However, this seems not to be the case. On average, employers report that 24 per cent of employees is 50 years of age or older. Compared to Eurostat's statistics on quarter 4 of 2009 this is similar to the EU average. In other words, the data does not contain an overrepresentation of relatively 'old' organisations, which might respond more to these kinds of questionnaires, but is a representative reflection in this respect.

Nevertheless, there could be other reasons giving rise to an unequally distributed non-response. In case one assumes a higher response among organisations holding negative stereotypes concerning older workers or having less confidence in a future with an ageing workforce, the results might be biased by employers 'ventilating' their discontent. In this case, results on behaviour are likely to underestimate recruitment and retention of older workers and positive perceptions, and overestimate negative perceptions. In case a higher response among 'good practice' organisations is assumed, results on behaviour are likely to overestimate recruitment, retention and organisational policies applied, while underestimating negative perceptions.

Overall, the maximum 'acceptable' level of non-response is hard to establish: as long as non-response is equally distributed there is —in principle— no reason for biased results. Furthermore, research suggests that in many cases surveys with varying response rates yield results that are statistically indistinguishable (Keeter *et al.*, 2006). Unfortunately, the previous reasons do not safeguard us from the possibility that the results are in fact biased.

1.5.2.   Case study research
Besides survey research, the ASPA-project also involved (longitudinal) case study research among organisations about the employment situation of older workers. In recent years, both at the EU level and in member states, research has aimed at identifying strategies and good practice examples which can help promote the integration of older people into the labour market (*cf.* Walker 1997; 1999; Walker and Taylor, 1998; European Foundation, 1999; Drury, 2001; Jepsen *et al.*, (eds.) 2002; 2003; Molinié, 2003; Lindley and Duell, 2006; Mandl *et al.*, 2006; Naegele and Walker, 2006). The selection of case studies aimed at revisiting long-established good practice examples from existing portfolios of positive examples. In other words: there was a focus on initiatives that had been in place for a longer period to be able to assess how they have developed over time. In this study, I use Dutch longitudinal cases to address the question how initiatives and organisational policies developed in the Netherlands over time, and how the economic climate and institutional changes have been affecting organisational practices aimed at extension of working lives of older workers.

1.6.   Outline of the book and research questions

This thesis consists of six chapters in total. Chapters 2 to 5 present the results of the study. These chapters are written as separate articles. Three articles (chapters 2, 4 and 5) have been published in international scientific journals; chapter 3 has been submitted for publication. Presenting the results in the form of separate articles has the advantage that chapters can be read independently of each other. A disadvantage is that part of the chapters will overlap. Overlap is particularly strong between chapters 4 and 5, since a number of conclusions presented in chapter 4 served as input for chapter 5.

Table 1.2 presents an overview of the content of the chapters. Chapter 2 takes an initial step towards the examination of possible changes in Dutch employers' behaviour regarding the recruitment and retention of older workers during the last decade and analyses surveys administered to Dutch employers in 2000, 2002, 2005, 2008 and 2009. The research question is:

1. Viewed over the last decade, to what extent have organisations been changing their recruitment and retention behaviour towards older workers and how can changes be explained?

Table 1.2. An overview of the content of the chapters

Chapter	Title	Key issues	Study design
1	Organisations dealing with an ageing workforce: views and behaviour across time and place	Background on ageing and the labour market in Europe; earlier research; theoretical considerations; data collection; research questions	Literature review
2	Are employers changing their behaviour towards older workers? *An analysis of employers' surveys 2000-2009*	*Changes over time:* changes in recruitment and retention behaviour; relative position of older workers compared to other groups; changes in organisational policies	Quantitative Dutch pooled cross-sectional data analyses
3	Ageing organisations and extension of working lives: a case study approach	*Changes over time:* effect of economic climate on organisational behaviour; effect of institutional changes on views and practices towards extension of working lives	Qualitative Dutch longitudinal case study analyses
4	Employers' attitudes and actions towards the extension of working lives in Europe	*International-comparative perspective:* recruitment and retention behaviour, perceived consequences of an ageing workforce; organisational policies; governmental policies	Quantitative internatinal-comparative survey research in organisations
5	Ageing and employers' perceptions of labour costs and productivity: a survey among European employers	*International-comparative perspective:* perceived changes in labour cost-productivity gap; determinants of perceived labour cost-productivity gap; effect of perceived labour cost-productivity gap on recruitment and retention behaviour	Quantitative interntional-comparative survey research in organisations
6	Employers' policies and practices towards extension of working lives: conclusion, discussion and implications	Conclusion, discussion and implications	

Essentially, the study distinguishes between two elements of a time effect and addresses the question: has employers' recruitment and retention behaviour been changing over time, and if so, has it been changing structurally or cyclically?

Whereas chapter 2 focuses on employers' recruitment and retention behaviour over time based on survey research, chapter 3 adopts a different approach in addressing changes over time: longitudinal case studies conducted among Dutch organisations are analysed. Chapter 3 examines views, dilemmas and behaviour from both the perspective of employers and older workers in an organisation over time. How do business-cycle effects and institutional changes affect for instance training opportunities for older workers, health policies, but also recruitment and retention levels? The chapter deals with how the economic climate and institutional changes have been affecting organisational practices aimed at extension of working lives of older workers over the last decade. The central research question is:

2. How have the economic climate and institutional changes been affecting organisational practices towards older workers over the last decade?

Chapter 4 and 5 address the international-comparative component of this study. In Chapter 4 the primary focus is on the examination of recruitment and retention behaviour towards older workers, employers' views on consequences of an ageing workforce, organisational policies, and what governments can do to extend working lives. The research question in this chapter is threefold:

3. What do employers consider to be the consequences of an ageing staff?
4. Do European employers take action to extend working lives and what organisational policies do employers apply to retain older workers?
5. According to employers — what can governments do to extend working lives?

A considerable share of employers turns out to associate the ageing of their staff with a growing gap between labour costs and productivity. Chapter 5 elaborates further on this perceived labour cost-productivity gap and studies the effects of tenure wages and employment protection on the perceived gap and whether perceptions affect employers' recruitment and retention behaviour towards older workers. The research questions in this chapter are:

6. What are the determinants of perceived changes in the labour cost-productivity gap due to the ageing of the workforce?
7. To what extent does the perceived labour cost-productivity gap affect employers' behaviour towards older workers?

Chapter 6 evaluates the answers to the research questions and discusses the scientific and societal relevance of the findings. Furthermore, the strengths and weaknesses of the study are reviewed and suggestions are made for future research.

2. Are employers changing their behaviour towards older workers? An analysis of employers' surveys 2000-2009[1]

Abstract
This study addresses possible changes in Dutch employers' behaviour regarding the recruitment and retention of older workers during the last decade. We analyse surveys administered to Dutch employers in 2000, 2002, 2005, 2008 and 2009. The results show that efforts to recruit older workers are changing, congruous with the economic climate, while retention behaviour shows a clear and rather gradual time effect. We conclude that the position of older workers has improved between 2000 and 2008 and has done so in comparison with other underrepresented groups in the labour market. During the recession, recruitment of older workers declined substantially, while efforts to retain older workers are in both absolute and relative terms higher than in 2000. With respect to organisational policies, the authors conclude that throughout the period under observation these policies are dominated by measures that 'spare' older workers.

2.1. Introduction

Raising the participation levels of older workers is one of the key objectives of policy makers in most Western countries (OECD, 2001). However, macroeconomic targets for increasing participation and increasing older people's working lives are unlikely to be met without employers' active support. There is still limited insight into how employers are behaving towards older workers, whether this behaviour is subject to change, and whether it is in line with those macro-level policies aimed at extending the working life (European Commission, 2004; 2005). Earlier research among employers, carried out in the United States and several European countries, shows that there is often a lack of corporate focus on older employees; this is reflected in an absence of programs to retain and retrain them (Barth *et al.*, 1993; Chiu *et al.*, 2001; Guillemard *et al.*, 1996; Henkens, 2005; Taylor and Walker, 1998; Van Dalen *et al.*, 2009; 2010). Furthermore, micro- and meso-level actors, including employers and employees themselves, seem to

---

[1] This chapter was published earlier as Conen W.S., C.J.I.M. Henkens and J. Schippers (2011), Are employers changing their behavior toward older workers?: An analysis of employers' surveys 2000-2009. *Journal of Aging and Social Policy*, 23(2), 141-158. Reprinted with permission from the Taylor and Francis Group.

hold a double standard towards increasing the number of older workers and postponing retirement; while agreeing that working longer may well become necessary in the future, workers and employers still do not think it will apply to them individually (Van Dalen *et al.*, 2009).

This situation raises several questions. Are employers responsive to all kinds of 'management by speech' from public officials and becoming more aware of the challenges ahead? And —an even more interesting question— do they behave accordingly? After all, Vickerstaff *et al.* (2003) have concluded earlier that any significant change in retirement behaviour will come primarily from policy modifications initiated and undertaken by employers. This study examines the behaviour of employers in retaining and recruiting older workers and will address three main questions:

- Viewed over the last decade, do employers' retention and recruitment behaviour towards older workers show any major changes?
- Compared to other underrepresented groups in the labour market, has the relative position of older workers in the 'job queue' been changing over the last decade? The 'job queue' (Thurow, 1975) refers to the idea of employers —who are in the process of recruitment and selection— ranking potential employees and placing them in a fictitious order of preference.
- Have organisational policies regarding older workers been changing over the last decade?

To answer these questions, we analyse the results of independent surveys among Dutch employers carried out in 2000, 2002, 2005, 2008 and 2009. In this study we make a distinction between two elements of a time effect: (1) *a trend effect or structural effect* and (2) *a business-cycle effect*. The first effect refers to a trend, or structural change, in the time period under observation. This trend effect indicates a fundamental change from the point of reference in a positive or negative direction. The second effect refers to an effect caused by changes in the business cycle. In our case it means, for example, that when the demand for workers changes, the demand for older workers changes as well.

2.2. Policy context

2.2.1. Reversing the exit culture: blocking pathways out of the labour market

Since the 1980s, the mobility of older workers has been dominated by exit mobility in the Netherlands. The three most important pathways out of the labour market have been early retirement, disability, and unemployment. From the 1990s onward, the Dutch government has concentrated on reversing the exit culture by blocking those exit routes. The first route the government attempted to close was the disability route, frequently used by employers to lay off workers. The measures taken have resulted in a strong decline in the inflow of workers into disability arrangements.

But the three pathways out of the labour market are not independent: closing one road results in more use of the other roads (Van Imhoff and Henkens, 1998). That is why in recent years the government, in its attempts to increase older workers' labour force participation, has also directed its attention to the other two exit routes: early retirement and unemployment schemes. Voluntary early retirement schemes, based on pay-as-you-go funding, have been transformed into actuarially neutral pre-pension schemes on a capital funded basis, and early retirement was further restricted by a new law in 2006. Both adjustments make if financially more attractive for older workers to prolong working life. Blocking unemployment schemes was addressed by reducing the maximum period of unemployment benefit entitlement and tightening rules on eligibility criteria.

Currently, the Dutch government is considering additional measures to reverse the exit culture. In 2009, plans were launched to raise the public pension age from 65 to 67 in about 2025. The way this increase will be realized (gradually, stepwise, or with a 'big bang') is still under discussion.

2.2.2. Age discrimination legislation

Age discrimination is one of the forces behind the phenomenon of the Dutch 'early exit culture'. Koppes et al. (2009) show that in the Netherlands age discrimination is perceived to be substantial: the self-reported rate of age discrimination in the category of older workers (55 to 64 years) is 20 per cent. As in other European countries, age discrimination laws in the Netherlands are of fairly recent date. In 2004, the government introduced specific regulation to combat age discrimination by enacting the Age Discrimination in Employment Act. This act prohibits discrimination based on age or behaviour that are the result of the difference in age in the field of labour.

The act applies to filling vacancies, employment finding, and the beginning or ending of labour relations. Someone who presumes to be a victim of age discrimination can request the Dutch Equal Treatment Commission to start an inquiry. The Dutch Equal Treatment Commission reports that about one-quarter to one-third of discrimination complaints refer to cases of age discrimination (Equal Treatment Commission, 2007).

2.2.3.   Trends in participation and unemployment rates

Looking at participation rates of adults between ages 55 and 64 over the years (see *figure 2.1*), policy makers might conclude that these rates gradually move to the 'right' direction. In 2001, the European Council defined a target for raising the average labour force participation of adults between ages 55 and 64 to 50 per cent by 2010 (European Council, 2001). Although the participation rate of Dutch workers aged 55 to 64 has increased substantially in recent years (47% in 2009), it is still below the target set.

Over the last decade, there have been both expansion and contraction in the Dutch labour market, as reflected in fluctuations of the overall unemployment rate (see *figure 2.2*). The period 2000 to 2005 was marked by growing unemployment, while 2005 to 2008 was a period of sharp contraction. In 2008, the unemployment rate was at a similar level as in 2000. Since

Figure 2.1. Labour force participation rate, period 2001-2009

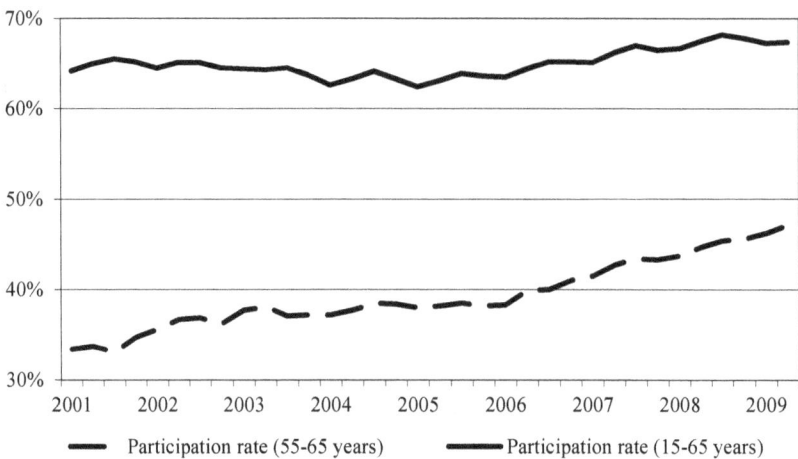

Source: Statistics Netherlands, 2009.

Figure 2.2. Unemployment rate, period 2001-2009

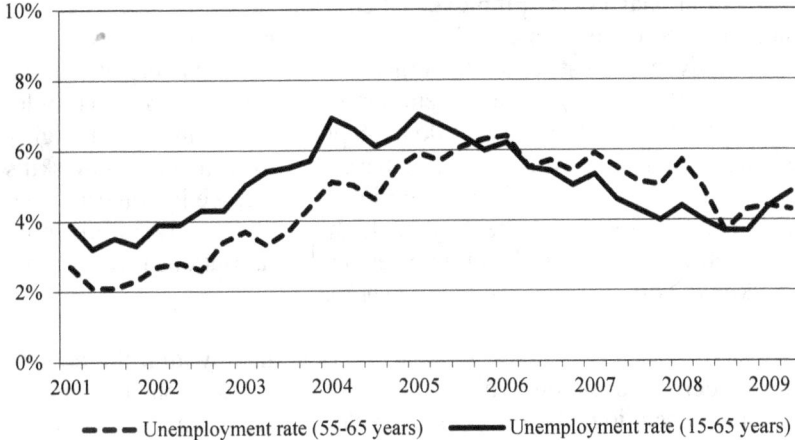

Source: Statistics Netherlands, 2009.

the beginning of the economic downturn in the second quarter of 2008, unemployment rates have been rising again.

Particularly when economic prospects are weak, older workers find themselves in a vulnerable position. Note in figure 2.2 that the unemployment rate of older workers remains relatively high for several years after the 'general' peak in 2005. This seems to underscore the idea that when there are enough 'other fish in the pond' older workers are among the last in the 'job queue'. Thus, their position still remains precarious during the period after an economic downturn, when younger workers already benefit from job growth.

The time frame of 2000 to 2009 thus provides us with the opportunity to analyse whether employers' behaviour towards older workers is affected by labour market fluctuations and corresponding perceived labour shortages or whether there is a more constant time effect.

2.3. Theoretical background

2.3.1.   Rational organisations and ageing
A basic tenet of organisational theory is that organisations are goal-oriented systems that strive for profit maximization, continuity, and a healthy market

position (Kalleberg *et al.*, 1996). These objectives could be described as basic organisational goals. Employers' behaviour towards older workers is assumed to be dependent on older workers' contributions in achieving these goals, given the restriction that organisations face. One organisational characteristic that may influence employers' behaviour towards older workers is the skill level required to do a job properly. Assuming that highly skilled and experienced workers are better equipped to acquire new skills and prevent their knowledge from becoming obsolete, we hypothesize that organisations that rely more heavily on highly skilled workers are more likely to recruit and retain older employees than organisations relying more on low-skilled workers (*human-capital hypothesis*).

The decision to retain or recruit older workers is made within the context of the broader organisation. This is not a static context, but one that is dynamically changing. Macro-level developments, such as economic changes, influence the choices made by managers. When organisations are shedding jobs as a result of an economic downturn or a declining demand for output, managers will be more pressured to implement cost-savings measures than in a favourable economic climate. We predict that perceived labour shortages will increase the likelihood of recruitment or retention of older workers (*business-cycle hypothesis*).

2.3.2.   Institutional isomorphism
The larger cultural and political contexts in which employers operate, or more generally the 'institutional surroundings', may play an important role in how employers behave towards older workers. In the theory of DiMaggio and Powell (1983), the notion of 'institutional isomorphism' (literally: taking on the same form or structure as another organism) identifies three mechanisms through which institutional change occurs: coercive, mimetic, and normative institutional isomorphism. Coercive institutional isomorphism stems from political influence and concerns the pressure exerted, either formally or informally, by other organisations, society's expectations, or by the government. Mimetic isomorphism results from standard responses to uncertainty and concerns the imitation of practices of other organisations. Normative isomorphism results from managers going to the same university or school, reading the same journals, going to the same conferences, and picking up the same ideas about what an organisation should be like; it concerns the professionalization of the organisation.

As stated before, during the last decade policy makers have preached the necessity to reverse the exit culture. Besides the more formal pressure we discussed in the political context, management by speech may also be interpreted as the kind of pressure that results in coercive institutional isomorphism. For example, in 2001, the Dutch Government installed the 'Taskforce on Older People and Employment' and, in 2005, the coordinating group 'Grey Works'. These initiatives relied to a large extent on management by speech; by giving lectures, calling work committees, advertising, and informing the press, they aimed at improving the employment prospects of older adults. A growing awareness of the ageing process may have changed the behaviour of employers in a positive direction, so that employers are gradually more likely to recruit and retain older employees within their organisations. The persistence of a time effect, even when controlled for business-cycle fluctuations, indicates a trend or structural effect. We hypothesize that, corrected for business-cycle effects over the period 2000 through 2009, employers have increasingly recruited and retained older employees (*trend-effect hypothesis*).

2.4.   Methods

2.4.1.   Data
The research questions will be answered using data from comparative surveys carried out independently among Dutch employers in 2000, 2002, 2005, 2008 and 2009. The questionnaires used in each of the five years contained similar questions on recruitment and retention measures, personnel policies, and features of the organisation. The names and addresses of the private sector organisations were taken from samples drawn from the trade register of the chamber of commerce. To include public-sector organisations, questionnaires were sent to organisations active in public administration and in the health and welfare sector. All questionnaires were sent by postal mail.

The total number of completed questionnaires amounts to 4,386, of which 1,016 are from 2000, 1,054 from 2002, 597 from 2005, 674 from 2008, and 1,045 from 2009. The total response rate ranged from 15 per cent to 36 per cent (see *table 2.1*), which is lower than the average response rate for individual surveys but in line with the rate generally found in corporate surveys. In Europe and the United States, response rates have been found to be 20 per cent to 30 per cent at most (see Brewster *et al.*, 1994; Kalleberg *et al.*, 1996). For the purpose of this study, we used 2,833 questionnaires completed by board members/managing directors (29%), owners (17%), plant managers (7%), and the heads of human resources departments (48%).

Table 2.1. Descriptive characteristics of samples used

Year	N	Response rate	N (Executives)	Sector distribution in the sample	Sector distribution according to Statistics Netherlands
2000	1016	36%	694	Industry and construction (29%) Service sector (30%) Public sector (41%)	Industry and construction (19%) Service sector (64%) Public sector (17%)
2002	1054	31%	697	Industry and construction (21%) Service sector (24%) Public sector (55%)	Industry and construction (20%) Service sector (63%) Public sector (17%)
2005	597	15%	282	Industry and construction (23%) Service sector (44%) Public sector (33%)	Industry and construction (19%) Service sector (62%) Public sector (19%)
2008	674	17%	367	Industry and construction (30%) Service sector (33%) Public sector (37%)	Industry and construction (21%) Service sector (63%) Public sector (17%)
2009	1045	23%	793	Industry and construction (33%) Service sector (31%) Public sector (36%)	Industry and construction (21%) Service sector (63%) Public sector (17%)

In table 2.1, these respondents are referred to as 'executives'. All relevant data have been merged to obtain a pooled cross-section data set.

Table 2.1 shows that data collection covered all sectors of the Dutch economy. Comparison with information from Statistics Netherlands revealed that the data are not representative for the sector distribution in each year. This has been corrected by taking 'sector' into account in the regression analyses and by attaching weights according to the population of organisations from Statistics Netherlands in the presentation of cross tabulations.

2.4.2. Variables and analyses

A pooled cross-section data set was used for the analyses. To answer the first research question, we performed multivariate logistic regression to analyse employers' behaviour towards older workers over the last decade. The dependent variable on retention behaviour was operationalized by asking respondents whether they encouraged workers to continue working until they reach age 65 ('1'currently applied, '0' not applied). Recruitment behaviour was operationalized by asking whether employers recruited older workers ('1' currently applied, '0' not applied). 'Older workers' were defined in the questionnaire as 'workers ages 50 years and older'. Descriptive statistics of the variables used in the analyses are presented in *table 2.2.*

In our models, the trend effect and business-cycle effect are separated in order to examine whether a possible time effect is either cyclical or structural in nature. For the trend effect, we constructed year dummies. To account for business-cycle effects, we included two variables: size changes and experienced labour shortages. The organisations' demand for labour is related to growth or contraction of the organisation. This is captured in the question of whether the number of employees changed in the last few years ('1' Yes, it grew; '2' No, it stayed (more or less) the same; '3' Yes, it contracted). Whether this demand for labour is being met is influenced by the external labour market. The degree of personnel shortages experienced was measured by asking respondents to what extent they encountered problems finding staff ('1' with a relatively large number of positions, '2' with some positions, '3' hardly ever).

To test the human-capital hypothesis, we included a breakdown of the workforce by level of education ('1' predominantly low-skilled, '2' predominantly medium-skilled, '3' predominantly high-skilled, '4' equally distributed).

Table 2.2. Descriptive statistics (N=2,833)

	Mean	SD	Min	Max
Dependent variables				
Recruitment				
Recruitment older workers (0=no, 1=yes)	0.18	0.38	0	1
Retention				
Retention older workers (0=no, 1=yes)	0.18	0.39	0	1
Independent variables				
Trend effect				
Year (2000 = reference category)				
2002	0.25	0.43	0	1
2005	0.10	0.30	0	1
2008	0.13	0.34	0	1
2009	0.28	0.45	0	1
Business-cycle effect				
Size change (contraction = reference category)				
Constant	0.34	0.47	0	1
Growth	0.50	0.50	0	1
Experienced shortages (no shortages = reference category)				
With some vacancies	0.49	0.50	0	1
With relatively many vacancies	0.22	0.42	0	1

Human capital

Educational level (predominantly low skilled = reference category)

Predominantly medium skilled	0.31	0.39	0	1
Predominantly high-skilled	0.14	0.29	0	1
Equally distributed	0.15	0.30	0	1

Control variables

Size of the organization (logarithm)	4.68	1.40	0.69	11.66

Sector of industry (public sector = reference category)

Industry and construction	0.31	0.46	0	1
Services	0.32	0.47	0	1

Share of workers older than 50 years (none = reference category)

1-9% of the workers older than 50	0.18	0.39	0	1
10-19% of the workers older than 50	0.28	0.45	0	1
20-29% of the workers older than 50	0.26	0.44	0	1
30% or more of the workers older than 50	0.23	0.42	0	1
Share female staff	36.68	28.05	0	100
Age of respondent	45.54	9.02	19	83
Gender of respondent	0.70	0.46	0	1

In addition, employment prospects of older workers may differ according to organisational settings (*e.g.*, size, sector, and gender or age composition) and personal attributes of the employers or managers (Henkens, 2005).

The control variables on organisational characteristics and characteristics of the respondent were assessed using six variables. To control for sector differences, respondents were given a list of industrial sectors defined by Eurostat (1990) and were asked to indicate the sector in which their own organisation operated. We categorized the sectors into 'industry and construction', 'services', and 'public sector'. Furthermore, respondents were asked for the number of male, female, and total number of employees; the share of female employees and the size of the organisation were derived from these questions. Fourth, the share of older workers aged '50 and older' was categorized in 2000 ('1' no older workers, '2' 1 to 9%, '3' 10 to 19%, '4' 20 to 29%, '5' 30% or more of workers over 50). For the years 2002, 2005, 2008 and 2009, when the 'share of older workers aged 50 and older' was a continuous variable, the number was recoded to the same categories. This variable has been transformed into a series of dummies. To account for possible differences in personal employers' attributes, we included age and sex as control variables in the analysis ('1' male, '0' female).

To answer the second research question, we examined the relative position in the job queue. This position was derived from the behaviour towards older workers as compared to other underrepresented groups in the Dutch labour market. Behaviour towards older workers was derived from the question of whether the organisation encouraged workers to continue working until they reach age 65 and whether employers recruited older workers ('1' currently applied, '0' not applied). The behaviour towards other eminent underrepresented groups is measured by asking whether employers recruited women, non-natives, and disabled or partially disabled people ('1' currently applied, '0' not applied).

To answer the third research question of whether organisational policies regarding older workers have been changing over the last decade, we measured policies aimed specifically at older workers. The questionnaires included several policy measures regarding older workers, including measures aimed at adjusting tasks and capabilities, enhancing work-leisure trade-off, and measures aimed at over-fatigue prevention ('1' currently applied, '0' not applied). The list of policy measures was based on an earlier study into age-conscious personnel policies in organisations (SZW, 1991).

2.5. Results

2.5.1.   Retention and recruitment behaviour

Table 2.3 presents the results of multivariate logistic regression analyses to explain employers' retention and recruitment behaviour towards older workers over the last decade. The odds ratio represents the ratio of the probability that employers retain or recruit older workers to the probability that they will not. The depicted odds ratio is a way of comparing whether the probability of a certain event is the same for different groups.

With respect to retention of older workers, the results show that organisations with a predominantly highly skilled staff are more inclined to retain older workers. This is in line with what one would expect from our human-capital hypothesis (*hypothesis: organisations that rely more heavily on high-skilled workers are more likely to recruit and retain older employees than organisations relying more on low-skilled workers*). With respect to the recruitment of older workers, the human-capital hypothesis is not supported.

Furthermore, the findings show that personnel growth in the recent past positively affects efforts in recruiting older employees and that the degree of personnel shortages experienced positively influences retention and recruitment behaviour. In other words, the business-cycle hypothesis is supported for both recruitment and retention (*hypothesis: labour shortages will increase the likelihood of recruitment or retention of older workers*).

It is noteworthy that despite that the unemployment rate rose during the period from 2000 to 2005, the efforts to retain older workers were not negatively affected. In 2008, the results showed a significant increase in employers' behaviour aimed at retaining older workers. In 2009, although the effect size was smaller than in 2008, employers were still more likely to retain older workers as compared to the year 2000. So, the data show a trend effect with employers being more supportive towards later retirement in their organisations. For recruitment, the results show that during the period from 2000 to 2005, efforts to recruit older workers declined significantly. In 2008, when the external labour market contracted, the results show an increase in efforts made by employers to recruit older workers. In 2009, efforts to recruit older workers declined significantly again. Overall, recruitment behaviour aimed at employing older workers seems to 'breathe' in accordance with the economic climate, and there seems to be no clear trend effect, indicating that employers in the Netherlands are becoming more inclined to recruit older workers. The trend-effect hypothesis is thus only supported in case of the

Table 2.3. Retention and recruitment of older workers (logistic regression analysis)

		Retention		Recruitment	
		Odds Ratio	Z-value	Odds Ratio	Z-value
Trend effect	Year (2000 = reference category)				
	2002	1.39*	1.99	0.81	-1.45
	2005	1.28	1.09	0.29**	-4.31
	2008	3.18**	6.81	1.30	1.63
	2009	2.10**	4.66	0.79	-1.56
Business-cycle effect	Size change (contraction = reference category)				
	Constant	0.92	-0.55	0.96	-0.21
	Growth	1.26	1.56	1.59**	2.94
	Experienced shortages (no shortages = reference category)				
	With some vacancies	1.34*	2.28	2.33**	5.76
	With relatively many vacancies	1.51**	2.62	2.17**	4.50
Human capital	Educational level (predominantly low skilled = reference category)				
	Predominantly medium skilled	1.31	1.68	1.04	0.25
	Predominantly high skilled	1.74**	3.02	1.37	1.71
	Equally distributed	1.46*	1.97	0.89	-0.59

Control variables				
Size of the organization (logarithm)	1.10*	2.55	1.10*	2.36
Sector of industry (public sector = reference category)				
Industry and construction	1.21	1.16	1.65**	2.91
Services	1.30	1.87	1.43*	2.43
Share of workers over 50 years (none = reference category)				
1-9% of the workers over 50	1.22	0.63	2.07	1.94
10-19% of the workers over 50	1.34	0.96	2.91**	2.87
20-29% of the workers over 50	1.72	1.76	3.15***	3.04
30% or more of the workers over 50	2.06*	2.32	3.86***	3.53
Share female staff	1.00	0.38	1.01**	3.12
Age of respondent	1.00	-0.52	1.00	-0.43
Gender of respondent	0.87	-1.22	0.69**	-3.22
Pseudo R^2	5.3		7.4	
Log likelihood	-1279.5		-1232.8	
χ^2	142.2		196.4	
N	2833		2833	

Note: *Significant at $p < .05$; ** significant at $p < .01$.
Dependent variable:do you encourage workers to remain employed till the age of 65? (1=yes, 0=no).
Dependent variable: do you recruit older workers? (1=yes, 0=no).

retention of older workers (*hypothesis: over the time period from 2000 to 2009, employers increasingly recruited and retained older employees*).

Besides, the results show that a higher share of workers older than 50 has a positive impact on employers' recruitment and retention of older workers. Finally, the results show that employers in 'industry and construction' and in 'services' are more inclined to recruit older workers than employers in the public sector.

2.5.2.   *Relative positions of underrepresented categories*

Employers may take different measures to deal with personnel shortages. In times when demand is high and the labour-supply pool is 'drying up', employers will become more creative and diverse in their actions to fill vacancies (*cf.* Henkens *et al.*, 2005). A number of target groups (women, older workers, non-native workers, and the disabled) are often identified as alternatives to the indigenous male labour force, which in many organisations traditionally constitutes the core of the workforce. From a job-search theoretical perspective (Phelps, 1970), employers associate each of these groups to a greater or lesser degree with higher labour or training costs —or lower expected benefits in terms of output— compared with the reference group of indigenous male workers. Based on these expectations, employers will rank members of different groups into a fictitious order of preference in the so-called 'job queue' (Thurow, 1975).

Increasing labour shortages may be beneficial not only for older workers, but also for other less preferred groups in the labour market. The question, however, is whether older workers have benefited more than other groups or —on the contrary— less. So, what has happened to the relative position of older workers in the queue as compared to other underrepresented groups in the labour market? And what has happened to the relative position of older workers during the current recession?

Table 2.4 summarizes measures applied by employers to counteract personnel shortages by year. Enlisted are the most eminent underrepresented groups in the Dutch labour market: female workers, older workers, non-native workers, and disabled and partially disabled workers. The results show that the recruitment of female workers, older workers, and non-natives and the reintegration of disabled and partially disabled workers followed the labour market pattern: between 2000 and 2005, we find a decrease in employers' willingness to hire these groups, while they became more attractive in 2008. The only exception to this pattern comes from the increase in employers'

Table 2.4. *Measures applied by employers in response to personnel shortages,*
2000-2009 (%)

Measures	2000	2002	2005	2008	2009
Recruiting more older workers	20	15	6	28	17
Encouraging workers to continue working until the age of 65	13	13	15	32	22
Recruiting more female workers	55	38	23	41	31
Reintegrating (partially) disabled workers	35	34	26	45	21
Recruiting more non-natives	*	33	23	43	21

Note: *Data not available.
Source: Employers' surveys, 2000, 2002, 2005, 2008 and 2009.

efforts in encouraging workers to continue working until age 65; this is the only dimension of employers' behaviour not following the labour-market pattern and showing a substantial increase over the years 2000 to 2008. In 2009, all recruitment and retention of personnel plummeted. However, the relative position of older workers caught up: the retention of older workers in 2009 was the second most applied measure, and, although lower than in 2008, the retention is relatively high compared to the period 2000 to 2005.

In relative terms, the results suggest that the position of older workers compared with those of female workers, disabled workers, partially disabled workers, and non-natives has improved over the last decade. However, older workers are still last in line when it comes to their recruitment.

2.5.3.   *Organisational policies*
Organisations can apply different sets of policies in order to retain older personnel. In *table 2.5*, policies are grouped into the following categories: measures to adjust tasks or capabilities, measures to balance work and leisure in a way more suitable to older workers, and measures aimed at preventing older workers from getting over-fatigued.

In 2009, 44 per cent of the employers applied ergonomic measures and extra leave opportunities for older workers. Least applied were measures to adjust tasks and capabilities. Measures in the area of over-fatigue prevention and work-leisure trade-off were applied two to three times more frequently than measures to adjust tasks and capabilities.

Table 2.5. Policies applied by employers in order to retain older personnel, 2000-2009 (%)

Measures	2000	2005	2008	2009
Adjusting tasks/capabilities				
Training programs for older workers	20	14	21	16
Demoting older workers to a lower rank and pay package	7	6	17	10
Work-leisure trade-off				
Part-time early retirement	35	39	46	42
Possibilities of extra leave for older workers	53	49	66	44
Long-term career breaks (*e.g.* sabbatical leaves)	8	8	15	*
Overfatigue prevention				
Decreasing the workload for older workers	36	31	42	36
Exemption from working overtime for older workers	32	29	39	*
Working time adjustments	45	28	38	*
Ergonomic measures	57	50	66	44

Note: Data not available for 2002. 'Data not available.
Source: Employers' surveys, 2000, 2005, 2008, and 2009.

In the period 2000 to 2009, results show that organisational policies 'breathed' simultaneously with the economic climate: a reduction of policies between 2000 and 2005, a revival in 2008, and a reduction in 2009 again. Part-time early retirement was the exception and showed a gradual increase during the period 2000 to 2008 and a small reduction in 2009.

Policies can be stimulating or permissive in nature. Overall, the higher levels of policies aimed at over-fatigue prevention and possibilities in the field of work-leisure trade-off suggest employers apply predominantly permissive policies regarding older workers. 'Activating' measures, such as training programs for older workers, are considerably less sought after by employers.

2.6. Discussion and conclusions

In this study, we have addressed three main questions: Have employers' retention and recruitment behaviour towards older workers been changing over the last decade? Has there been a change in the relative position of older workers in the 'job queue' as compared to other underrepresented groups in the labour market? And, have organisational policies regarding older workers been changing? To answer these questions we analysed employers' recruitment and retention behaviour and compared organisational policies for the years 2000, 2002, 2005, 2008 and 2009.

Both retention and recruitment behaviour of employers have been changing markedly over the last decade, though in different ways. Employers retention behaviour showed a clear and rather gradual time effect between 2000 and 2008: there was a significant increase in the number of employers encouraging workers to remain employed until age 65, even when changes in labour demand and experienced shortages were taken into account. During the recent recession, there has been a strong decline in efforts to retain older workers, but still the retention level is high when compared to the period 2000 to 2005.

When it comes to employers' recruitment behaviour, we see a different picture. In the period 2000 to 2005, efforts to recruit older workers declined significantly, following the pattern of a rise in unemployment rates. In 2008, employers were more inclined to recruit older workers than they were in 2005, again following the development of unemployment rates. In 2009, employers' efforts to recruit older workers declined significantly again. Overall, recruitment behaviour seems to change parallel to the economic climate. Despite the improvement of the relative position of older workers compared to other underrepresented groups in the Dutch labour market —female workers, non-native workers, and disabled and partially disabled workers— there is no indication that employers are becoming more favourably disposed to recruit older workers.

Employers predominantly take permissive measures regarding older workers. Generic policy measures that seek to accommodate older workers, for example, offering them additional leave, are often perceived and put into practice as 'age-conscious' personnel policies. The paradox of this type of age consciousness is that these actions seem in fact to limit the opportunities of the older worker in the Dutch labour market (Euwals *et al.*, 2009). Employers are especially sceptical about the application of measures imposed by government or sector-wide labour agreements because these measures reduce older workers' employability and raise costs. Very few organisations have personnel policies targeted at narrowing the growing productivity-wage gap. So, although there is a growing tendency of employers to encourage older workers to continue working until age 65, this behaviour goes hand-in-hand with policies that imply a rather passive role for older workers.

The obstacles faced by older workers are not a typically Dutch phenomenon. These obstacles are found in many Western European countries, as shown in the OECD report *Live Longer, Work Longer* (2006). The Netherlands differs from other countries, however, because the labour costs of older employees are high and incumbent employees are relatively well-protected, which reduces their labour-market mobility. The paradoxical situation is that older workers occupy quite different positions in the Netherlands: the insiders hold a rather strong position, but outsiders —those who want to (re) enter the labour market— hold a weak position. This constitutes the crux of the policy dilemma that advanced welfare states, especially in Europe, have to deal with. One aspect of employment protection —income security and the seniority principle— stands in the way of the other aspect of protection -giving the unemployed reasonable chances at finding jobs.

This study has a number of limitations. One is its reliance on self-reported behaviour. It is possible that respondents report recruiting or retaining older workers in accordance with dominant organisational or national policies but do not comply. Future studies may combine self-reported behaviour with direct measures of hiring and retention behaviour. Another limitation is that respondents are mainly recruited among 'higher management', such as board members, managing directors, owners, plant managers, and heads of human resources. There may be a gap between what these higher managers think is happening in their organisations and what is actually happening in day-to-day business. On the one hand, one can argue that higher management is well-informed and has the best insight into the policies and organisational behaviour. On the other hand, one can argue that higher management may have a limited view on practices in lower levels of the organisation; people who are closer to the 'real world' may provide other and maybe more reliable outcomes.

It remains to be seen whether the current economic recession obstructs the process of especially retaining older workers. The first pleadings to re-establish voluntary early retirement schemes have been already uttered in the Dutch media. The Dutch still carry their legacy of 'the early exit culture', meaning that many employers share the opinion —and they are no exception to the large majority of Dutch people— that many older workers have 'paid' their share and are entitled by now to a well-deserved period of rest and retirement. This inheritance of the early exit culture is also reflected in the fact that although the statutory retirement age is 65, very few workers (fewer than 20%) reach that age while still in the labour force. Employers contribute to this early exit culture: many older workers would have worked longer if retirement had not been forced on them (Van Solinge and Henkens, 2007). From this perspective, the intention of the Dutch Cabinet to raise the statutory age of retirement from 65 to 67 reflects high ambitions; Dutch employers and employees seem to be not even used to the idea of working till age 65.

3. Ageing organisations and extension of working lives: a case study approach

This study examines how the economic climate and institutional changes have been affecting organisational practices aimed at extension of working lives of older workers over the last decade. We analyse longitudinal case studies conducted among Dutch organisations. Our findings show that during economic downturns organisations cut expenses, leading to a decrease in training budgets, recruitment levels and retention practices. Institutional changes regarding early retirement arrangements and the debate about raising the official retirement age have made both employees and employers realise that extension of working lives has become an actually unavoidable fact, although both parties still seem intrinsically opposed. Preferences to extend working lives appear to be primarily supply-driven, depending on the financial pressure felt by and the wants and capabilities of the individual worker. Employers seem to be able to find creative short-term solutions when necessary, although they also feel they have to put up with problems resulting from government policies for which they do not have a solution. Incited by pressure of safety regulations and the costs involved for the employer in case of drop-out, the case studies show an increasing focus on health-related measures in professions with intense physical work over the last decade.

3.1. Introduction

Under the influence of rising life expectancy and declining birth rates, the process of population ageing is taking place in almost every country across the globe (UN, 2007). In European countries, the ageing of societies will pose major challenges for public policy to cope with a declining labour force and rising welfare state expenditures (European Commission, 2006). Furthermore, although in the short run the current economic crisis enlarges labour pools, in many European regions a decrease in effective labour supply is expected in the long run. Policy makers are therefore increasingly paying attention to the labour market situation of older workers (OECD, 2001; European Commission, 2006) and scholars have started to focus their attention on organisational practices and policies towards older workers.

Earlier survey research among employers, carried out in the United States and several European countries, shows that there is often a lack of corporate focus on older employees, reflected in an absence of programs to retain and retrain them (Chiu *et al.*, 2001; Guillemard *et al.*, 1996; Henkens,

2005; Taylor and Walker, 1998; Van Dalen *et al.*, 2009a; 2010b, Conen *et al.*, 2012). Conen *et al.* (2011) find that employers' efforts to recruit older workers are changing congruous with the economic climate, but retention behaviour shows a clear and rather gradual positive time effect over the 2000s. These studies show that although in general the corporate focus on older workers is rather low, employers seem to be gradually changing their behaviour towards older workers. While such survey research addresses questions on incidence and trends in organisational practices in general, it does not deal with ambivalent developments and underlying motivations (for instance, when an organisation reports to have measures to maintain older workers' health in 2000 and 2010, the content may still have changed considerably under influence of various factors). We approach changes in organisational practices aimed at extension of working lives from a different perspective by using longitudinal case study research. In our research, a case study refers to a study of a corporate setting with the intent of getting to a holistic understanding of behaviour towards extension of working lives, using a number of different research methods (unstructured interviews, semi-structured interviews and desk research).

Earlier case study research with an emphasis on the organisation focuses on identification, drivers and dimensions of good organisational practices in age-conscious personnel policies (Walker and Taylor, 1998; Walker 1999; Taylor, 2006; Frerichs *et al.*, 2012) and stereotypes and age-group relations (Brooke and Taylor, 2005). Case study research regarding exit pathways and continuity of employment examines older workers' constraints, career trajectories and retirement decisions in organisations (Vickerstaff *et al.*, 2003; Vickerstaff, 2006a; 2006b; Brooke, 2009). Taylor *et al.* (2010) examine continuity of employment by addressing the perceived fit between employees of different ages and their employing organisations. In this study we contribute to previous research on ageing organisations by examining a topic that to our knowledge has not been studied before: how have changes in the economic climate and in the institutional surroundings been affecting organisational practices aimed at extension of working lives over the last decade?

To answer this main research question, we selected cases from existing databases examining ageing organisations in the early 2000s, and revisited these 'good organisational practices' in 2010 to establish longitudinal case studies. Case study research offers the possibility to take into account the existence of contrasting or complementing views on developments in organisational practices. In our study, we seek to explore organisational behaviour from the perspective of both management and employees. As stated by Vickerstaff (2006a): "Too often research on organisational practice remains at the level of policy documents and the espoused policy of management" (p. 508). Previous research shows that intended organisational policies and policies as perceived by employees may differ (Edgar and Geare, 2009; Khiji and Wang, 2006). Yin (2009) points out that a common concern about case studies is how to generalize from a case. He states that "…the case study, like the experiment, does not represent a 'sample', and in doing a case study, our goal will be to expand and generalize theories (analytic generalization) and not to enumerate frequencies (statistical generalization)" (p. 15).

The time frame of our longitudinal case study research allows us to examine why and how employers' behaviour towards older workers has been evolving, since the first decade of the 21st century is a period with apparent labour market fluctuations and institutional changes in the Netherlands. In 2005 unemployment was at its highest level. The period between 2005 and 2008 was very prosperous, but then the financial crisis hit in 2008, resulting in higher unemployment rates in 2009 and 2010.

The article is structured as follows. In section 2 and 3, we address respectively the policy context and theoretical background regarding organisational behaviour towards older workers. Next, an introduction to the methodology employed in the study is provided. The results are presented in section 5, and in section 6 we conclude with a summary and discussion.

3.2. Blocking the exit routes

During the 2000s, the Dutch Government has been concentrating on reversing the exit culture by blocking various pathways out of the labour market. A first major route that the Government attempted to close was the disability route, a route that was frequently used by employers to lay off workers. The Netherlands' Bureau for Economic Policy Analysis calculated that in 1998 nearly one-third of men in the age category of 55 to 64 received disability benefits (Centraal Planbureau [CPB], 2000). Since the 1990s, disability benefits have been reduced, the criteria to enter a disability scheme have become more restrictive and several penalties have been introduced to discourage employers from 'dumping' workers. The sickness period paid by the employer instead of the government was expanded and new legislation introduced in 2002 increased the obligations of employers and employees during the first two years of illness, with full responsibility for employers to take care of sick leave support and reintegration, and the responsibility of employees to cooperate. Financial sanctions follow in case either party does not live up to this obligation. In 2004, the period of sick pay to be complied by employers was extended from a maximum of 52 to 104 weeks. A new law stimulating employers and employees financially to reintegrate partially disabled workers was introduced in 2005. Furthermore, the working conditions act contains regulations for employers and employees to enhance health, safety and welfare of employees, and is aimed at prevention of work-related injuries and illness. In 2005 and 2007 adjustments were made to the act, bringing Dutch regulation more in line with European directives and decentralising policy making from the government level to the organisational level (Ministry of Social Affairs and Employment, 2012).

Furthermore, substantial alterations were made in voluntary early retirement schemes. The schemes used to be based on pay-as-you-go funding and have been transformed into actuarially neutral pre-pension schemes on a capital funded basis after the middle of the 1990s. Most pre-pension schemes were designed in such a way that an employee needed to work for 40 years to obtain a full allowance. At the introduction of pre-pension schemes older employees often were offered transitional arrangements, containing guarantees of the age at which they were allowed to stop working or the height of the allowance. In 2006, early retirement was further restricted by a new law. These adjustments make it financially more attractive for older workers to prolong working life. Although workers in most sectors of industry can still use early retirement schemes if they want to, this usually comes at greater costs.

In 2009, plans were launched to raise the public pension age from 65 to 67 in about 2025. The way this increase has to be realized (gradually, stepwise, or with a 'big bang') has since been under heavy discussion in the country. In the beginning of 2012, the members of the House of Representatives have given their consent on a legislative proposal to change the official retirement age to 66 in 2020 and 67 in 2025. In April 2012, the cabinet resigned and a few days later the caretaker government accepted the Stability Programme. This programme states to raise the retirement age stepwise, starting in 2013. In 2019, the retirement age will be 66 and 67 in 2024. After this, the retirement age will be interlinked with life expectancy (Government of the Netherlands, 2012).

3.3.   Theoretical background

A basic tenet of organisational theory is that organisations are considered to be goal-oriented systems that strive for profit maximization, continuity, and a healthy market position (Kalleberg *et al.*, 1996). These objectives could be described as basic organisational goals. Organisational behaviour towards older workers is assumed to be dependent on older workers' contributions in achieving these goals. Although organisations may not be able to take all alternatives and consequences of an action into account, we assume they will strive towards rationality in their decision-making. Organisational behaviour towards older workers is influenced by the context of the broader organisation. This is not a static context, but one that is dynamically changing. Macro-level developments, such as economic changes, influence the choices made by managers. When organisations are shedding jobs as a result of an economic downturn or a declining demand for output, managers will be more pressured to implement cost-saving measures than in a favourable economic climate. We expect that *business-cycle effects* will affect the likelihood of employers stimulating older workers to extend working lives.

Rational organisations, however, might also be concerned with long term sustainability of their staff. Although in the short run the current economic crisis enlarges labour pools, organisations may look beyond the crisis and anticipate to a period with an expected decrease in the effective labour supply. In that light, it would be rational for employers to pay increasing attention to practices and policies towards older workers and stimulate extension of working lives.

From an institutional economic perspective, the larger cultural and political contexts in which employers operate, or more generally the 'institutional surroundings', may play an important role in how employers behave towards older workers. Whereas the previous paragraph outlined the major changes in public policies, in our findings we focus on the perception and interpretation of those policies. The mechanism of 'institutional isomorphism' (DiMaggio and Powell, 1983) may have changed behaviour in a direction in which employers and employees are gradually more aware of and more likely to adjust to extension of working lives. We expect employers and employees to have found *institutional effects* to be increasingly present during the 2000s, but we don't know how the implemented policies are perceived by employers and employees and how institutional changes have affected their behaviour.

3.4. Methods

The case studies conducted were part of the 'Activating Senior Potential in Ageing Europe' project (ASPA). We conducted longitudinal case studies to explore how personnel policies towards older workers evolved during the last decade and to explain why employers' behaviour towards older workers changed. To that aim, we selected good practice organisations from existing databases (European Foundation, 2006; Grey Works, 2006; 2007), and revisited these former case studies between March and October 2010 to establish a longitudinal case study. The three case study organisations in this study are from distinct industries and contain robust information on both managerial practice and employees' views and experiences. Characteristics of the organisations are as follows:

1. The first organisation is a public sector police organisation. The organisation employs workers in physically demanding professions as well as white-collar workers. In 2010 the organisation employed around 4,800 workers, which is an increase of approximately eight per cent since the early 2000s. Within the force, 67 per cent of employees is male. In the recent past, the organisation has received orders to reduce headcount. The organisation is active in a highly urban area of the Netherlands. A total of 15 participants were interviewed. Key informants from this organisation included middle and upper levels of management, career advisor, HR officers and employees.
2. The second organisation is a private sector organisation in the construction industry, employing mostly skilled manual workers. The organisation is in a competitive industry. In 2010, the firm employed around 90 workers and is rather constant in headcount over the 2000s. Almost 90 per cent of the employees is male. A total of nine key informants were interviewed. The interviewees were from middle and upper levels of management, HR management and employees.
3. The third organisation is an IT-services company with a highly educated professional and managerial staff. The organisation is in a competitive industry. In 2010, the firm employed around 30 workers, a decrease of approximately 10 per cent in the 2000s. About two-third of employees is male. Interviews undertaken yielded a total of 21 informants. The interviewees in this case were from various levels of the organisation including the director, middle management and employees.

All three organisations have a history of early retirement (as do almost all organisations in the Netherlands), but in the 2000s these organisations were awarded for their human resource policies regarding older workers and extension of working lives. We predict that changes in the business-cycle and institutional surroundings have similar effects on the organisations under examination. This is in line with what Yin (2009) calls literal replication logic: we use three organisations to confirm (or reject) inferences drawn on business-cycle effects and institutional effects.

We distinguished eight categories of measures of employers' behaviour towards older workers, based on Frerichs and Lindley (2009). During the case study research, we examined what areas were covered at the time of the original case study and compared this to the areas covered during the revisit. *Table 3.1* shows an overview of developments in the action areas covered in the three organisations categorised by stage of professional association. The table shows varying combinations of measures aimed at extension of working lives, between 4 and 6 measures. Applied measures appear constant

Table 3.1. Areas of employers' behaviour towards older workers (50 years and older), in three longitudinal case study organisations, categorised by stage of professional association

	Construction		IT-services		Public sector	
	t1	t2	t1	t2	t1	t2
Recruitment						
Job recruitment	*	*	*	*		
Maintenance and development						
Training, lifelong learning and knowledge transfer	*	*	*	*	*	*
Career development and mobility management					*	*
Flexible working practices			*	*	*	*
Health protection/promotion and workplace design	*	*	*	*	*	*
Retention and exit						
Redeployment and retention	*	*			*	*
Employment exit and transition to retirement				*		*
All phases						
Remuneration						

Notes: t1 = present during original case study; t2 = present during revisit.

over time in these organisations, except for the recent developments in the area of employment exit and the transition to retirement.

In total, we used interviews from 45 respondents: 6 HR officers (including career advisor), 12 middle and higher managers, and 27 employees. We conducted unstructured interviews, semi-structured interviews and desk research on policy documents, internal studies and memos, minutes, organisational newsletters, and former case study materials. An interview guideline as well as a common template for reporting and assessing the individual case studies was developed. In all three organisations, unstructured interviews were held with one higher manager on the topic of policies and practices towards older workers, and then semi-structured interviews were conducted with the other respondents. Semi-structured interviews addressed: (1) organisational background, workforce and environment; (2) the rationale and context of the original measures; (3) the development of the original measures and current practice; (4) general age-management approach; (5) any other business, contact details and finalizing the interview. Transcripts of interviews, field notes and desk research materials were imported into a software package for data storage, retrieval and analysis (WeftQDA). The analysis was carried out with the help of this program as interviews were reread and coded along the lines of: business-cycle effects, categories of institutional contexts (*e.g.* disability regulation, early retirement/extension of working lives) and various types of organisational practices (*e.g.* practices in the field of health and safety, training, flexible working practices).

3.5.   Results

3.5.1.   *Business-cycle effects*
Over the last decade, organisations have been making decisions on older workers' retirement age in both times of prosperity and during economic downturns. In this section, the main question is whether the economic climate affects organisational behaviour aimed at extension of working lives. The first stage of a professional association between employers and older workers is the hiring procedure. Interviewees in all three case study organisations indicate business-cycle effects play a role in recruitment behaviour towards older workers. Economic downturns decrease the likelihood of recruitment of older workers, and the opposite holds for times of prosperity.

A representative narrative of a 59 year old construction manager shows how recruitment of older workers is related to business-cycle fluctuations:

"Twelve years ago, it was really hard to find someone. The only ones we could get were in fact those older employees. And they were older workers we knew. So we approached them to come and work for us. And they still do."

Employers seem to base their hiring decisions on implicit or explicit cost-benefit computations. Interviewees sometimes narrate in terms of implicit computations, like considering absenteeism, physical constitution, skill level, previous education and past employment. A construction manager mentions that initially fixed-term temporary contracts are offered to older workers, which is in a way an approach to check whether the implicit computation proves correct. The director (46 years) from the IT-services organisation tells explicitly about costs and benefits. He positively states about the productivity of an older worker:

"You just say 'Look [name of older worker], this is your cabinet, these are the accounts, this is our software, okay, these are your passwords'. Ready. He sits down and gets to work. While when you hire a younger applicant without such experience, then you need to explain everything."

But he also emphasises concerns about costs:

"[Hiring an older employee] makes a difference for the rate of pension contributions, health care costs and absenteeism insurance. Those get a little more expensive with age. On a whole salary, it's about six per cent annually. It's not about thousands, or, well, it is about thousands, but not so many thousands that it would be a reason not to hire someone. That's when you look at the total costs —I am sorry, I am an employer— that's what you get, you start looking at what someone costs."

Subsequent to the hiring stage, productivity maintenance and development is a central theme in an older workers' career. Extension of working life is often perceived to be stimulated by lifelong learning, because learning is assumed to enhance productivity — also at older ages (European Commission, 2006; OECD, 2006). In all three organisations, considerations in the form of training initiatives, learning-on-the job routines, mentoring concepts and knowledge transfers from older/retiring employees to younger employees (or vice versa) seem to be rather consistent over time. Many quotes on this topic indicate time-consistency on the *existence* of policies, and are of the form: '… because we always did it like that'. But the *extent* of putting these initiatives into practice actually seems to depend on the economic climate. In all three organisations, managers put forward that during economic downturns expenses were cut and this also led to a reduction in employability resources.

Training budgets have become tighter, and downturns lead to different forms of learning. These cutbacks seem to have a direct effect on formal ways of training. A 58 year old manager at the police department says during the interview:

"There are financial constraints. A Personal Development Plan can partly exist of training on-the-job and partly of theoretical education. Theoretical education is impossible with the current budget cuts, that is almost 'not done'. Maybe for some individuals, a real high-potential, you can manage to arrange something at the moment. But that is the current time-frame, which will probably pass by."

Another police manager says:

"The work needs to be done as well. So you have to strike a balance, in how much room there is in terms of budget and in terms of time to have people trained. And I don't think training is the only way to develop."

Not only formal training is under pressure, but also other ways of learning, such as training-on-the-job by transferring knowledge from older to younger workers. A 45 year old manager at the construction firm describes how their organisation lets older workers purposefully work together with young workers as their mentors, to facilitate the transferring of knowledge and skills. But he also states:

"Well, when shortages arise in budgets and all, then you turn to completely different processes of course. Unfortunately with us, we had to as well. Because we have to be highly competitive in the market at the moment, our mentors for instance have less time to train their apprentices."

Flexible working practices such as working time arrangements or facilities to reconcile work and family life or care are seen as another important instrument for retaining older workers in employment (Naegele and Walker, 2006). Flexible working practices are implemented in the IT-services organisation and the police department, but not in the construction firm. There is no indication from our case studies that flexible working practices are related to business-cycle fluctuations: the application of a flexible approach seems to be time-consistent.

The last stage in a professional association between older workers and an organisation includes retention and the transition to retirement. Changes in the economic climate also seem to affect these areas.

A 45 year old manager at the construction firm sketches the situation of their organisation around 2006, when the economy was recovering fast and the work 'exploded':

"At that time we had two 62 year olds, and we had a high pressure on production. So we thought 'why are we letting go two fine contractors, when we need them so much?' And the men liked to be involved as well; they did not want to sit at home. So we asked them to continue working. We had to fix two things actually, in the short run we needed capacity and besides that we needed mentors."

In 2010 the economic climate has changed considerably and interviewees describe how this leads to different attitudes towards extension of working lives. For instance, the police department has received orders to reduce headcount significantly in the years to come. Whereas retention of older workers used to be the most prominent thought on their minds, the thought on early exit as a solution to the problem of necessary staff reductions seems to return easily. A career advisor (58 years) tells:

"While in the past we used to say 'we are going to take measures to keep employees and their qualities on board', we now have completely different interests because we simply need to reduce costs. This also means people over 60 years will probably be offered the opportunity to leave early. The younger ones, born after a certain date, fall under other arrangements and will be transferred internally or externally. But the reasoning is based on economics rather than ideology at the moment. It is simply a budget cut."

3.5.2.   Institutional context
In this section we examine how institutional changes in 1) health and safety regulations and 2) regulations concerning early retirement and the retirement age have been affecting views and practices towards extension of working lives.

Health and safety
During the 2000s, the costs involved for employers in case their employees call upon the sickness benefits act have increased substantially, making disability leave a bigger financial problem for employers than it used to be. The influence of institutional surroundings on employers is reflected by the comments of a construction firm manager (59 years):

"You can push until he [the employee] breaks down and then he will call upon the sickness benefits act. You as an economist understand: that costs money, and we as non-economists understand that as well, because we have to pay them."

"And that is of course the topicality [extension of working lives], you hear about it everywhere, and all kinds of important issues, but what is discussed less is how exactly are we going to keep the men outside healthy until they are 65, later 66, 67?"

Especially in the organisations with intense physical work (*i.e.* construction firm and police organisation) health-related institutional forces are likely to shape organisational behaviour towards extension of working lives. In the IT-services case study organisation —a company with a highly educated professional and managerial staff— interviewees and documents do not indicate a focus on health-related measures. In both the police department and the construction firm, there has been a clear increasing focus on health protection and promotion. In the police organisation, several programmes, facilities and tests have been implemented for employees to stay hale and hearty over the years. Tests in place cover for instance shooting skills, self-defence and violation control. The organisation started to offer facilities to test your physical fitness and to provide advice and support to increase fitness. During the last decade, programmes were disentangled for younger and older employees, as a 46 year old employee explains:

"When you are 55+ years, now, old folks follow an adapted physical training. Even for me, when I have to sport with a youngster, they easily dislocate my arm; they handle things more roughly and are more fanatical."

Initially, most of these health practices were on a voluntary basis. Later, some tests became obligatory, but the results were only indicative. In the near future, some tests will become obligatory and staff will be facing consequences in case they fail to meet targets. Moreover, several pilot programmes were started, involving a track of filling in a questionnaire and discussing the outcomes with a company doctor, who will give advice on for instance diet, rest or exercising, and a pilot with measuring blood values for half a year.

A significant increase of health-related practices is also visible in the construction organisation. Whereas health and safety-related behaviour used to be voluntary in the early 2000s, considerable standardization changes have taken place since. For instance, employees used to receive general clothing allowance but did not always buy proper clothing with it, so from halfway the 2000s onwards employees receive free work wear, while retaining their clothing allowance. Also the quality of work clothing has improved considerably. The behaviour to actually wear the clothing is stimulated by regulations, as expressed by a 51 year old construction worker:

"I see workers wear their safety clothing. You have to, because when the health and safety inspectors [ARBO] come to visit, they will send you away and it gives trouble; also for the boss of course, because he has to pay the fine. That is a waste of money of course. Recently, I also see workers from other firms wear their safety clothing."

Furthermore, employees report to have an extensive physical examination by a company doctor every two years. Also, there has been an increasing focus on the use of tools and materials to relieve heavy work, and stricter maxima of carrying weights. Also this behaviour is at least partly stimulated by institutional forces, as a construction manager (59 years) explains:

"When something is less heavy and easier to handle, he [the employee] is more productive. So, often it is just an investment that is recovered soon. It is also an investment to prevent drop out. Drop out costs also 40,000 a year, yes, 2 years say 80,000 Euros. Than it is better to invest 10 or 15 thousand Euros in better equipment. We may be unable to read or write, but arithmetic we do well."

Early retirement and retirement age
During the 2000s, substantial alterations were made in the institutional context to make it financially less attractive for older workers to withdraw from the labour market early. Although workers in most sectors of industry can still use early retirement schemes if they want to, this usually comes at greater costs. Whereas the transitions in the disability regulation became apparent around the middle of the 2000, the alterations in the early retirement schemes have come into effect gradually and are of more recent date. Our study reveals that in all three organisations, employees have fairly corresponding views on the relationship between institutional changes in retirement arrangements and the last career phase. In general, the institutional changes regarding early retirement and the debate on extension of working lives have made workers realise that extension of the individual's working life is increasingly becoming an inevitable fact of life, although employees do not seem too enthusiastic about it:

"Extension of working lives beyond 65? I think it is an outrage! I mean, doing this work for more than 40 years, that's outrageous. They don't suffer from it, right, they sit in an office on their lazy butts and they can make the decisions. That is what I sometimes think. At one point it stops [physically], of course. And then you have nothing. Just some unemployment benefits." (Older worker, construction firm, 65 years)

Employees predominantly report external pressure in the form of financial repercussions in case they do not extend their working lives, but appear intrinsically opposed to the changes.

Some employees still fall under transitional arrangements and are 'safe' from recent policy reforms. The following quote from an older construction worker (59 years) is typical in this respect:

"I am not going to work until 65! Certainly not. No, I will continue until December next year. For financial reasons I would continue working, but I don't have to."

A one year younger worker (58 years) at the police department can also retire early, but considerably later than the construction worker:

"With my arrangements I think I can retire at age 62. But when I do, I lose a lot of money compared to when I retire at 63. So I am calculating and thinking about the amount of money I want to receive after retirement."

In general, employees interviewed were not disliking their work. On the contrary, after stating the unfairness of the obligation to extend working lives, many workers indicated on a second note that if they had to continue working they would not really mind to prolong their current profession, as long as their constitution would allow them. The opposition to extend working lives rather seems to originate from the feeling of injustice, the fear of an increasing probability of productivity difficulties, and the personal financial disturbance the changes can bring. Employees in that respect also acknowledge employers' interests may be quite opposite to their own. A white-collar employee (58 years) at the police department describes this situation in his interview as a 'peculiar paradox':

"For me as a person for instance, it has become very unattractive to retire early, financially, and they made it exceptionally attractive to stay, financially. And at the same time they say to me: we would like you to leave".

But not only employees feel 'overpowered' to extend working lives, also employers are not necessarily keen on finding ways to keep workers employed. Sometimes they feel put up with problems for which they do not have a solution. A career advisor (58 years) of the police department formulates it this way:

"Early-, late-, night shifts are heavy. If you think people should extend their working lives, then you have to look carefully at what tasks those people actually can do. And how to make sure the young ones will not get burned-out? I don't know the answer to that question, but that is almost a question for the government to solve. Because they say "extent working lives" and we are supposed to fix this? It has major consequences..."

And a manager at the police department:

"The formations are getting smaller and you have the same amount of work to do with less staff. Ageing continues. When you ask me: "How to solve this?" Then I will answer: "You need a magic trick". Because there are many smart people who say this is insolvable."

Nevertheless, the choice to extend working lives is a question employers in all our three case studies principally leave to the wants and capabilities of the individual employee and therefore largely seems to be supply-driven. The following quote of a construction manager (59 years) is representative in that respect:

"I have one [employee] who is 60, 61 and he does not want to quit. He says: "I will continue until the age of 65". And his mate is 58 and he says: "if I've got the money tomorrow, I will put my bum under a palm tree". And I say: "I come and sit with you if I've got enough money tomorrow!" Because it's as simple as that. They started the whole discussion about extension of working lives, but they did not think it through."

Given the seemingly unavoidable fact that extension of working lives has become, does this also mean that organisations have started initiatives to moderate this extension? All three organisations seem to have developed a different approach towards older workers when it comes to extension of working lives. At the IT-services case study organisation, this phase does not have a special place in interviewees' minds. Flexible working practices are the dominant solution in all stages of life (parenting, informal care, work-life balance in general), and therefore also considered appropriate practices for older workers. The transition to retirement is for instance optionally seen in a reduction of working hours before retirement. A white-collar employee at the IT-services organisation (62 years) says:

"There is an option to work less days a week, and adjust time if you want. That is also convenient for instance for older workers."

At the construction firm, redeployment and retention is a central element of their behaviour towards older workers, encapsulated in a long-term vision on how to behave towards workers at all stages of life. The general idea at the firm is that: employees rotate jobs throughout the whole career, the organisation invests in equipment and developments of lighter materials, and if necessary workers are 'spared' for a while (regardless of age). This view is confirmed by managers and employees themselves and seems to have been constant over time. An illustrative quote comes from a manager (59 years):

"We always looked for redeployment. We have a builder working in an administrative function, we have a paver working a crane and another one is riding a truck."

Finally, the police case study organisation has adopted a completely different approach, by focusing primarily on the final phase as such. There is a strong focus on reduction of working hours, which is anchored in personnel policies especially for employees of 55 years of age and older. People close to retirement are asked what they want to do in their last few years within the organisation and how the organisation can facilitate this. The way the three case study organisations handle the question on how to 'add a few years' differs depending on their general ideology, but all in all the three employers seem to be able to find creative short-term solutions when necessary.

A final question is what will happen to arrangements designed to 'spare' older workers, such as shift exemptions and extra leave, due to institutional changes. Documents and interviews do not indicate any major change in policies for senior workers yet, but the following quote from a manager at the police department addresses the difficulties employers see themselves faced with if they pursue sparing arrangements:

"We have a government that told us to extend working lives. If people of 55 years and older can ask for night shift exemption, what happens if 40 per cent of your staff gets 55 years and older? Ageing. They all ask for nigh shift exemption and you have to grant that request. Personnel policies for older workers, okay, fine with me. But can you tell me who is going to do the night shifts?"

3.6. Conclusion and discussion

In this study we examined how the economic climate and institutional changes have been affecting organisational practices aimed at extension of working lives over the last decade using longitudinal case studies. The results show that business-cycle effects play a substantial role in organisational behaviour towards older workers, for instance in terms of the crisis negatively affecting training budgets, recruitment behaviour, retention practices and extension of working lives. Employers do not seem to be inclined to look beyond the current economic crisis — a period of possible labour market shortages. Their focus is on the current situation and not on the long run. Incited by safety regulations and the costs involved for the employer in case of drop-out, the case studies show an increasing focus on health-related measures in heavy professions over the last decade. Institutional changes regarding early retirement arrangements and the debate about raising the official retirement age have made both employees and employers realise that extension of working lives has become an actually inevitable fact, although both parties still appear intrinsically opposed. Several ingredients seem to play a role in employees' opposition to extension of working lives, such as feelings of injustice, the fear of an increasing probability of productivity difficulties, and an anticipation of increasing personal financial pressure to extend working lives. Furthermore, employees anticipate employers' interests to extend working lives may not match their own interests. Preferences to extend working lives seem to be primarily supply-driven, depending on the financial pressure felt by and the wants and capabilities of the individual worker. Employers in our case study organisations are able to find creative short-term solutions when necessary, e.g. in redeployment and initiatives to add a few years, although they also feel they have to put up with consequences for which they do not have a solution. So, even though neither employers nor workers endorse public policies to extent working lives and raise retirement ages wholeheartedly, employers and workers do comply.

This case study research contributes to research on organisational behaviour towards extension of working lives in several ways. First, it gives insight into changed content of umbrella concepts. Whereas for instance training provisions and health-related measures in organisational longitudinal survey research may report to exist constantly over time, the *extent* and the *content* of practices in this area seem to have evolved substantially. It is very difficult to capture the complexity of such umbrella concepts in survey research. Furthermore, the choices and constraints both managers and employees face regarding extension of working lives are complex and shifting. Business-cycle fluctuations and changes in the institutional framework interact with organisational behaviour, and such mechanisms are difficult to capture in survey research. The use of multiple case studies with both the perspective of managers and employees sheds light on several attitudes and processes resulting from institutional changes in health-related regulations and regulations concerning retirement. We find that adaptations in health-related regulations have lead to marked changed behaviour in organisations in order to meet the new regulations, and the necessary changes are supported by both managers ánd employees. Regarding changes in early retirement and the retirement age we find more ambiguous attitudes and behavioural changes in the organisations. In our study, extension of working lives seems to follow a bottom-up process and is characterised by a rather reactive stance of employers.

Nevertheless, being a case study approach, the results are to be interpreted analytically and cannot be generalised statistically. The organisations under study were selected as and can still considered to be good practice organisations. Therefore, it may very well be the case that whereas employees and managers in these organisations do find opportunities to extend working lives, individuals in other organisations may have less influence on their timing and manner of retirement. The degree of choice individuals face in their voluntariness of retirement decisions has been examined in previous research (cf. Isaksson and Johansson, 2000; Dorn and Sousa-Poza, 2005; Solinge and Henkens, 2007). These studies find a substantial degree of involuntariness in retirement decisions (on average circa 25%). Our findings suggest that employers and employees do realise that extension of working lives has become an inevitable fact. How to achieve the desired goal —a later time of retirement— is now for employers and employees to fill in. Institutional changes are likely to have a significant impact on prolongation of careers, but that does not answer the question *how* to keep older workers functioning in a maximally productive way. In the organisations under study, practices towards extension of working lives still seem to be in their initial stages. Future research may want to focus on understanding the practices applied by employers and establish what kind of practices are beneficial to sustainable extension of working lives.

4. Employers' attitudes and actions towards the extension of working lives in Europe[1]

Abstract

Although policymakers have put great efforts into the promotion of older workers' labour force participation, quantitative empirical knowledge about employers' views towards extension of working lives is limited. The purpose of this study is to improve the understanding of employers' attitudes and actions towards extension of working lives, by examining recruitment and retention behaviour towards older workers, employers' views on the consequences of an ageing workforce, organisational policies, and what governments can do to extend working lives. The authors analyse surveys administered to employers in Denmark, France, Germany, Italy, the Netherlands, Poland, Sweden and the UK in 2009. The results show that a minority of employers have applied measures to recruit or retain older workers, and employers rather retain than hire older workers. A considerable share of employers, albeit to different degrees per country, associate the ageing of their staff with a growing gap between labour costs and productivity. Employers expecting a larger gap do not apply more organisational measures to either increase productivity or adjust the cost-productivity balance. Employers may think the cost-productivity issue is partly for governments to solve; employers expecting a larger cost-productivity gap consider wage subsidies to be an effective measure to extend working lives.

4.1. Introduction

The ageing of society and the workforce is one of the dominant developments in modern Europe. Although in the short run the current economic crisis enlarges labour pools, in many European regions a decrease in effective labour supply is expected in the long run. Moreover, the ageing of society will cause rising welfare state expenditures (European Commission, 2006). Therefore, according to governments and experts, nations and labour markets are in need of higher participation rates of older workers and working lives need to be extended.

---

[1] This chapter was published earlier as Conen W.S.,K. Henkens and J.J. Schippers, 2012, Employers' attitudes and actions towards the extension of working lives in Europe. *International Journal of Manpower*, 33(6), 648-665. Reprinted with permission from Emerald Group Publishing Limited.

Over the last decade, older workers have been gradually working both longer and more (Eurostat, 2010). Despite these upward-sloping participation trends, in most countries employment rates still drop considerably for workers between ages 55 and 59, dropping sharply after age 60 (see *table 4.1*). Furthermore, the mean and median age of retirement are often well below the statutory age of retirement — in other words, in most countries early retirement is still rather the rule than the exception. One such exception is Sweden, which is performing relatively well in retaining older workers for the labour market.

Although early retirement may be the rule, older workers' labour force participation rates vary considerably between European countries. There are several explanations for these differences —which are not necessarily mutually exclusive— such as institutional arrangements affecting both supply and demand for older workers and employer and employee attitudes and behaviour towards extending working lives. Vickerstaff *et al*., (2003) state that any significant change in retirement behaviour will come primarily from policy modifications initiated and undertaken by employers. This study therefore examines the role played by employers in the recruitment and retention of older workers.

To what extent are employers active players in the current process away from early exit and towards extension of working lives? Earlier research among employers, conducted in the USA and European countries, shows that many employers tend to be biased towards older workers, and there is often a lack of corporate focus on older employees that is reflected in an absence of programmes to retain and retrain them (Barth *et al*., 1993; Chiu *et al*., 2001; Guillemard *et al*., 1996; Henkens, 2005; Taylor and Walker, 1998). The main questions we will address in this study are:

- Do employers take action to extend working lives in terms of recruitment and retention of older workers?
- What do employers see as possible consequences of an ageing workforce for their own organisation?
- What organisational policies do employers apply to retain older workers?
- And —according to employers— what can governments do to extend working lives?

This study is among the first to address employers' attitudes and actions with respect to the extension of working lives from a cross-national perspective. We analyse data from comparative surveys carried out among employers in

Table 4.1. Employment rate, life expectancy and retirement age

	EU	Denmark	France	Germany	Italy	Netherlands	Poland	Sweden	UK
Employment rate (2009)									
50-54 years	75.0	84.1	80.5	79.6	69.9	82.2	68.1	84.3	79.2
55-59 years	60.0	78.5	58.5	70.2	50.7	72.4	42.6	80.3	70.6
60-64 years	30.4	36.6	17.0	38.7	20.3	37.3	18.2	60.5	44.9
Part-time employment (2009)									
50-64 years	19.6	22.6	18.8	27.2	10.6	47.3	12.1	25.4	27.9
Life expectancy at age 65 (2007)									
Males	17.0	16.5	18.4	17.4	18.0	17.1	14.6	17.9	17.5
Females	20.5	19.2	23.0	20.7	21.8	20.7	18.9	20.8	20.2
Mean age of retirement (2005)									
Males	61.4	61.2	58.5	61.4	60.7	61.6	62.0	64.3	63.4
Females	60.4	60.7	59.1	61.1	58.8	61.4	57.4	63.0	61.9
Median age of retirement (2005)									
Males	60.7	62.2	58.8	61.6	58.4	60.5	57.0	63.9	63.8
Females	59.4	60.1	58.3	59.9	57.2	59.3	55.2	63.3	60.3

Source: Eurostat (2010).

Denmark, France, Germany, Italy, the Netherlands, Poland, Sweden and the United Kingdom. These countries cover all types of European welfare state regimes as proposed by Esping-Andersen (1990). Employers from different countries face different labour market and institutional restrictions and policies set out by their governments. This may influence their behaviour on how to deal with the consequences of an ageing workforce. It may also influence their ideas on who is primarily responsible for the consequences of an ageing workforce.

The article is structured as follows. Section 2 discusses the theoretical background from the employers' perspective on dealing with an ageing workforce. Section 3 describes the data and variables used in this study. Our results are presented in section 4, and section 5 presents our main conclusions and discusses the outcomes.

4.2.   Theoretical background

4.2.1.   Ageing, productivity and labour costs

According to economic theory, employers' considerations on how to assess the future with an ageing workforce are based on the expected relative benefits and costs of employing workers of different age groups. If wages of older workers exceed their productivity, these are workers representing a potential loss for firms. Examining the relationship between age, labour productivity and labour costs often starts from human capital theory (Becker, 1962; for an overview, see Polachek and Siebert, 1993), which states that investments in human capital boost labour productivity and productivity is positively related to employee remuneration. In principle, people accumulate human capital by training and experience during the whole of their career, which translates into increasing remuneration over time. However, human capital also may depreciate, e.g. because knowledge of older technologies becomes obsolete or because cognitive and physical skills deteriorate. Depreciation of human capital will lead to a decrease in productivity. To balance costs and benefits —from a traditional neo-classical theoretical perspective— remuneration should decline accordingly.

In the late 1970s doubts accumulated about the empirical validity of relationship between age, labour costs and productivity as described by human capital theory (Hutchens, 1989). Lazear (1979) was among the first to address issues such as why do jobs exist where wages increase with seniority, regardless of improvements in productivity. His delayed payment contract theory illustrates how employers may have implicit contracts with their employees regarding the connection between productivity and income over a lifetime: earnings are lower than productivity during the first phase of workers' careers and higher during the second phase. Such contracts function as an incentive for employees to put enough effort into their work to obtain the higher wages at the end of the implicit contract period. An employee who shirks runs the risk of being fired before the wage premium is obtained. Hence delayed compensation works as an incentive for employees to work harder, stay longer with the organisation and transfer human capital to younger generations of workers.

Skirbekk (2008) provides an overview of how age impacts the various physical and cognitive skills of workers, and how this translates into changes in productivity potential. Many studies find that productivity tends to reach a peak in mid-career, roughly somewhere between ages 30 and 45 (*e.g.* Lehman, 1953; Ilmakunnas *et al.*, 2004; Jones, 2005). Productivity depends on both physical and cognitive skills, and the impact of age on both types of skills has been studied extensively. Looking at physical skills, the biological process of internal depreciation is irreversible, although inter-individual differences are considerable. In general, a decline sets in from age 30 onwards, but because this is a very slow process and because most organs have overcapacity, most people only signal problems from age 60 onwards. Starting from age 45, many people notice that their physical condition is deteriorating. Older workers tend to have longer recovery periods. Physical skills obsolescence is particularly important in manual jobs and often related to unskilled jobs (Hidding *et al.*, 2004; Nauta *et al.*, 2004). In modern societies, cognitive skills have gained significance and have become a strong predictor of productivity. Although it is generally accepted that physical abilities decline with age, cognitive functioning has more ambiguous outcomes. Cognitive functioning is often divided into fluid and crystallised cognitive functioning (Horn and Catell, 1967; Baltes *et al.*, 1999). Fluid cognitive skills refer to the process of acquiring information, like mental agility, mental arithmetic, solving problems and making quick connections. The quality is genetic and comes with high inter-individual variation. These skills decrease with age. Crystallised cognitive skills refer to knowledge and experience that is embodied in a person after years of practice, learning and repeating. These skills are found to increase with age. In addition, older workers often compensate lower fluid cognitive skills by using adaptation strategies (Baltes *et al.*, 1999). Until recently, crystallised skills have received little attention in age-related cognitive research.

Although the age-productivity profile is hard to observe and generalise, we expect employers to have some idea about the relative productivity of older workers as compared to other age groups. Such ideas may be based for instance on employers' observations of personnel over time and comparisons with other staff members. Employers also know the context and the extent to which older workers are able to keep up with job requirements when they age. This is related to what Phelps (1972) calls 'previous statistical experience': information on how certain categories of employees tend to behave and develop. Many employers use these statistical experiences to formulate expectations regarding the future productivity of employees who belong to a particular category.

4.2.2.   Policies to extend working lives

Most European employers realise that an ageing workforce may result in future labour market problems (Van Dalen *et al.*, 2009). Given this awareness and the attempts of European governments to address topics such as raising the retirement age and stimulating older workers' labour force participation, employers may anticipate and thus apply measures that will facilitate an extension of working lives. Organisational policies towards extension of working lives are based on the profitability of this action, therefore labour costs and productivity can be considered to be important determinants. The logical thing to do for employers is thus to take measures aimed at reducing the labour cost-productivity gap, by, first, enhancing productivity, second, balancing costs and productivity or third, reducing labour costs. This means employers may take measures aimed at maintaining workers' human capital to prevent an eventual decline in productivity (*e.g.* training plans for older workers) or aimed at bringing back the wage-productivity balance (*e.g.* by means of demotion). Training plans and demotion, when applied thoughtfully, are often mentioned as a potential solution to expected negative consequences of an ageing workforce (Hall and Isabella, 1985; European Commission, 2006). In order to reduce labour costs, a possible solution to face negative consequences of an ageing workforce is to let go of 'expensive' staff members, such as older workers enjoying relatively high seniority-based wages or older workers with decreased productivity and no remuneration adjustments. Early retirement schemes can therefore be considered a way to reduce labour costs. If employers do not see any options to reduce the gap, they may turn to finally, accommodative measures to prevent a further decline and preserve workers' current productivity. In this category we find policies such as decreasing the workload for older workers, extra leave for older workers or reduction of working time before retirement.

The state of the economy may affect employers' attitudes and behaviour towards older workers. Employers in countries with low unemployment rates (like the Netherlands, at about 4-5%) are more likely to recruit and retain older workers and to apply measures stressing the importance of extending careers than employers in countries with high unemployment rates (like France, Sweden and Poland, with unemployment rates between 8 and 10%).

4.3. Methods

We used data from comparative surveys carried out among employers in Denmark, France, Germany, Italy, the Netherlands, Poland, Sweden and the United Kingdom. Participating research institutes in the ASPA project carried out the data collection. ASPA is an acronym for 'Activating Senior Potential in Ageing Europe', a research project funded as part of the EU 7th Framework programme under the Socio-Economic Sciences and Humanities theme. Data collection took place from March to November 2009. The total number of completed questionnaires amounts to 5,822, of which 609 are from Denmark, 500 from France, 892 from Germany, 770 from Italy, 1,077 from the Netherlands, 1,037 from Poland, 525 from Sweden and 412 from the UK (see *Appendix A.1*). The overall response rate was 23 per cent and ranged from 7 to 53 per cent for the various countries. This is lower than the average response rate for individual surveys but in line with the rate generally found in corporate surveys. In Europe and the USA, response rates have been found to be 20-30 per cent at most (see Brewster *et al.*, 1994; Kalleberg *et al.*, 1996).

The questionnaires used in the different countries were identical, and were translated from English to the national languages. The national questionnaires were checked by the overall co-ordinator on international comparability before the fieldwork started.

The surveys were sent to directors, owners and heads of HR departments. Interview techniques used differed between countries, depending on what was perceived to be the best way to address respondents in a specific country. Denmark did computer-assisted web interviewing; Germany, the Netherlands and Sweden used paper and pencil; and France, Italy, Poland and the UK did computer-assisted telephone interviewing.

For all countries we drew a stratified sample on the sector and size characteristics of the establishments. In the analyses at the national level we weighted the data afterwards to account for the sampling design, to ensure the observations were representative for the population of employers. Weights were constructed according to the population of establishments from national statistics bureaus and corrected for sector and size of the establishment. To present results at the pooled level, we pooled the data for all eight countries —including the national weighting factors— and constructed a new weighting factor that takes the net sample size of the different countries into account. Otherwise, Dutch and Polish employers (N>1,000) would influence results more than French and Swedish employers (N≈500).

4.4. Results

4.4.1. Retention and recruitment behaviour

The first results we present, show —for all countries— that employers rather retain than recruit older workers (*table 4.2*). At the pooled level, 12-13 per cent of European employers recruit older workers or employees who already retired during a personnel shortage; 27 per cent encourage older workers to continue working until retirement age. The retirement age seems to be a normative barrier in all countries, because very few employers stimulate working beyond the statutory retirement age by either recruiting or retaining older workers. For instance, 27 per cent of European employers stimulate working until the statutory retirement age, whilst 13 per cent stimulate working beyond the retirement age. Another more general feature seems to be that none of the measures to recruit or retain older workers have been applied by a majority of employers. On average, only 2 per cent of employers apply all four measures we asked for to either recruit or retain older workers and 63 per cent indicate neither recruiting nor retaining older workers.

The results also show some differences between countries. Polish employers display the most activating behaviour: 5 per cent apply all measures asked for and 39 per cent neither recruits nor retains older workers. Recruitment of retirees is generally low, but Poland is an exception in this respect, as recruitment of retirees is rather common there. Polish and French employers report most often stimulating older employees to continue working until the official retirement age. This may find its origin in the fact that French and Polish employees retire relatively early. Italian and Dutch employers exhibit the least activating behaviour, with considerably lower levels of recruitment and retention of older workers than in other countries.

Table 4.2. Recruitment and retention behaviour towards older workers (%)

	Pooled	Denmark	France	Germany	Italy	Netherlands	Poland	Sweden	UK*
Stimulate working until retirement age	27	34	40	26	11	17	40	27	-
Stimulate working beyond retirement age	13	18	8	7	5	8	26	15	-
Recruit older workers	12	16	11	22	2	10	15	12	-
Recruit employees who already retired	13	8	10	17	3	4	38	7	-
All of above recruitment/ retention measures	2	2	1	3	0	0	5	2	-
None of above recruitment/ retention measures	63	57	54	56	82	75	39	66	-

*Note: Data from the UK is not available, because a shorter questionnaire was used that did not cover the questions on recruitment and retention behaviour

Source: ASPA Employers Survey (2009)

Although cross-national differences are clearly present, an important finding is that recruitment and retention levels of older workers all over Europe are rather low in general. This seems to indicate that, on a more aggregated level, employers may be reluctant to actively promote older workers' employment by either hiring them or encouraging them to continue working until retirement age — let alone beyond retirement age.

4.4.2.   Age, productivity and labour costs

Employers' behaviour towards older workers may stem from various underlying reasons, such as the expected consequences of an ageing staff for their own organisation. *Table 4.3* sets out how employers expect an ageing workforce will affect productivity and labour costs. With respect to the relationship between ageing and productivity the results show that in all countries a majority of employers state that productivity as such is not affected by an ageing workforce. However, a substantial minority (28%) expects productivity to decrease: this is the highest in Germany, where 38 per cent of employers expect a productivity decline, and at 15 per cent lowest in the UK. On the other hand, on average ten per cent of employers expect productivity to increase.

A positive effect of an ageing workforce can be seen in the second part of the table, presenting employers' expectations regarding the knowledge base. Roughly half of employers expect an increase in the knowledge base, and 10 per cent expect a decline. When combining employers' opinions on the development of productivity and on the knowledge base one may conclude that from the employers' perspective an increasing knowledge base does not seem to directly translate into higher productivity. Even though human capital increases, the additional human capital is not necessarily relevant from the perspective of productivity.

The third part of the table presents the expectations regarding the influence of ageing on labour costs. Lazear's theory on implicit contracts contends that it is a decline in productivity which is behind a lack of support for working longer. It is in the nature of the contract that workers are paid more than they are 'worth' at higher ages, even when productivity remains the same. The table offers some support for this notion. For the pooled sample we established that almost half of employers expect an increase in labour costs[2]. There are, however, large differences between countries. In Poland,

---

[2]   Labour costs may consist of both direct wages and additional labour costs (such as extra leave or sickness absenteeism). Although "wages" and "labour costs" are not the same, in the economic literature it is more common to talk about a wage-productivity gap than about a labour cost-productivity gap. We therefore use "wages" and "labour costs" interchangeably.

Table 4.3. *Expected consequences of an ageing personnel structure for own organisation (%)*

Consequences	Pooled	Denmark	France	Germany	Italy	Netherlands	Poland	Sweden	UK
Labour productivity									
(Strong) increase	10	10	7	10	14	8	10	8	11
Same	62	71	64	54	62	58	61	55	74
(Strong) decline	28	19	28	36	25	34	29	37	15
Knowledge base									
(Strong) increase	42	47	53	46	38	45	26	46	42
Same	49	44	42	43	52	49	65	42	52
(Strong) decline	9	9	5	11	10	7	9	12	6
Labour costs									
(Strong) increase	44	33	51	48	49	75	16	44	34
Same	52	61	43	51	48	24	74	50	62
(Strong) decline	4	6	6	1	3	1	10	6	3

Note: Based on the question: 'If the average age of your personnel increases by 5 years, what will be the effect on [...]?'
Source: ASPA Employers Survey (2009).

Denmark and the UK up to one-third of employers expect labour costs to increase. In Sweden, Germany, Italy and France roughly half of employers expect costs to increase. Employers in the Netherlands are at the other end of the spectrum: here 75 per cent think labour costs will increase due to an ageing workforce. Only very few employers expect a decline in labour costs, with Poland leading at ten per cent.

The combination of expectations on labour costs and productivity translate into expectations on the development of the labour cost-productivity gap with an ageing workforce. We combined the answers given in table 4.3 with respect to labour costs and labour productivity to establish whether employers perceive a cost-productivity gap as a result of an ageing workforce. For instance, when an employer expects an increase in labour costs accompanied by a decrease in productivity, this indicates an increasing cost-productivity gap. The same holds for a situation in which productivity is expected to stay the same but labour costs are expected to increase; this will imply an increase of the cost-productivity gap. *Figure 4.1* shows the results of this categorisation.

Figure 4.1. Employers' expectations with respect to the labour cost-productivity gap with an ageing staff

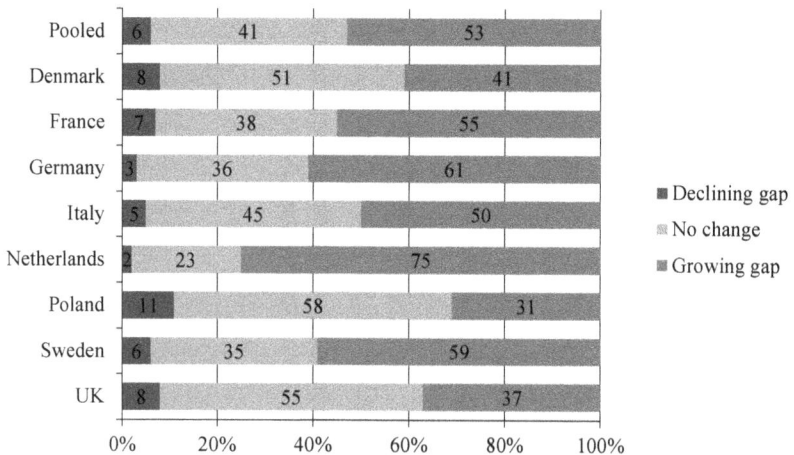

Source: ASPA Employers Survey (2009).

Overall, about half of employers expect the wage-productivity gap to increase with an ageing workforce (53%). The table shows large differences between countries. Dutch employers are most sceptical when it comes to expectations about older workers; 75 per cent expect the wage-productivity gap to increase as the workforce ages. In Poland and the UK the wage-productivity gap is less of an issue; in those countries about one-third of employers think the wage-productivity gap will increase.

4.4.3.   Organisational policies

An important question is how these employers' expectations regarding the wage-productivity gap translate into organisational policies. Are policies focused on bringing costs and benefits of older workers into equilibrium? Even if in the past employers' behaviour did not indicate an emphasis on activating behaviour with respect to recruiting and retaining older workers, maybe current policies do show a path towards activating behaviour and thus towards extension of working lives? To answer such questions, we presented employers with a list of measures and asked them to indicate whether their organisation was currently applying them. The list was based on earlier research into age-conscious personnel policies (e.g. Remery et al., 2003)[3]. As mentioned in section 2, organisational policies are categorised into four categories. The first category aims to enhance productivity (training plans for older workers), the second can be considered as a way to reduce labour costs (early retirement), the third focuses on balancing costs and productivity (for instance by reducing both tasks and salary, or demotion) and the fourth category is a group of 'accommodative measures' (such as possibilities for extra leave or decreasing older workers' workload). Table 4.4 presents an overview of the share of employers from different countries that apply different measures.

In general, employers most frequently implemented flexible working hours as a measure aimed at accommodating the needs of older workers (35%). Organisations in several countries, like the Netherlands and Denmark, do take various measures, such as reducing the workload or offering possibilities for extra leave. Lifelong learning is often perceived to be the key solution to enhance productivity at older ages (European Commission, 2006; OECD, 2006). The share of organisations offering training programmes for older staff varies highly between countries, but is on average about one-quarter. Relatively many UK employers report having training plans for older

---

[3]   In earlier studies we allowed employers to also come up with 'other' measures that were not included in the list of suggested measures. All additional measures mentioned by employers could easily be classified under the heading of the measures already included in the list.

Table 4.4. Policies implemented by employers in order to retain older personnel (%)

	Pooled	Denmark	France	Italy	Netherlands	Poland	Sweden	UK
Productivity								
Training plans for older workers	23	7	46	2	8	37	7	49
Costs								
Early retirement schemes	17	6	18	6	32	33	11	1
Balance costs - productivity								
Reduction in task and salary (demotion)	7	10	3	1	3	4	2	22
Accommodative measures								
Extra leave	15	26	9	1	31	3	8	14
Decreased workload	18	24	9	6	25	11	12	23
Reduction of working times	23	34	8	2	20	4	21	48
Ergonomic measures	29	28	28	5	28	38	32	30
Flexible working hours	35	NA	28	12	32	29	42	NA

Source: ASPA Employers Survey (2009).

workers. French employers also applied training plans relatively often; this may stem from the inter-sectoral agreement on 'employee lifelong access to training' adopted in France, which promotes training among experienced workers and was signed in 2003 by the French social partners (OECD, 2006).

Early retirement schemes, which can be considered a way to reduce labour costs for employers, are implemented by 17 per cent of European employers. In the Netherlands and Poland about one-third of employers apply early retirement schemes. It is obvious that higher levels of early retirement schemes do not stimulate the extension of working lives, and the higher levels of Dutch and Polish employers do not reflect a focus on career extension. Measures aimed at reviewing older workers' productivity and remuneration, such as reduction in task and salary (demotion), were found to be almost absent, with the exception of the UK, where 22 per cent of employers implemented this policy. The results from table 4.4 thus show that in most countries training plans and demotion —although often suggested by scientists and policy makers to tackle negative consequences of an ageing workforce— are not embraced by employers.

In *table 4.5* we present the results of a multivariate analysis conducted to examine employers' policies towards older workers in more detail. We looked at four types of policy measures:

1. Training plans for older workers (to increase labour productivity);
2. Early retirement schemes (to reduce labour costs);
3. Reduction of tasks and salary, or demotion (to balance productivity and costs); and
4. Reduction of workload (same as demotion, but without remuneration adjustments).

We tested whether personnel policies undertaken by employers are related to the expected wage-productivity gap. In the model we included country dummy variables as well as structural characteristics of the organisation, such as sector, age structure, skills level and size as control variables. In table 4.5 the odds ratio represents the ratio of the probability of employers applying a measure to the probability they will not.

Do employers who expect a larger wage-productivity gap take measures more often to bridge this gap than employers who are less concerned with this gap? Table 4.5 shows that employers expecting a larger gap do not more often attempt to enhance productivity through training or to balance cost

Table 4.5. Organisational human resource policies (logistic regression analysis)

	Training plans for older workers		Early retirement schemes		Reduction of tasks and salary		Reduction of workload	
	Odds ratio	Z-value	Odds ratio	Z-value	Odds ratio	Z-value	Odds ratio	Z-value
Expected wage-productivity gap	0.96	-0.81	1.17**	3.16	1.03	0.36	1.12*	2.10
Sector of industry (public sector = reference category)								
* Industries and construction	0.78*	-2.44	1.52**	4.33	1.01	0.07	0.81*	-2.16
* Services and trade	0.90	-1.00	1.13	1.16	1.32	1.86	0.69**	-3.42
Size of the organisation (logarithm)	1.30**	9.49	1.59**	16.99	1.36**	8.83	1.28**	9.55
Skills level of workers								
Share of employees in high-skilled jobs	1.50**	2.67	1.18	1.15	0.91	-0.39	1.14	0.85
Share of employees in unskilled jobs	0.74	-1.90	0.67**	-2.55	0.68	-1.61	1.19	1.11
Share of older workers	1.95**	2.81	5.32**	7.36	1.44	1.01	1.38	1.35
Countries (Sweden = reference category)								
Denmark	1.03	0.17	0.76	-1.52	7.08**	7.27	4.06**	8.26
France	11.30**	11.75	1.75*	2.44	0.78	-0.47	0.91	-0.37
Germany	3.45**	7.06	1.54**	2.71	1.26	0.77	0.70	-1.83
Italy	0.20**	-5.53	0.57**	-3.21	0.23**	-3.10	0.58**	-2.75
Netherlands	1.45*	2.09	6.60**	12.62	2.09**	2.70	4.04**	8.66
Poland	6.06**	10.90	4.41**	10.02	0.89	-0.35	0.92	-0.43
UK	11.73**	12.97	0.06**	-4.85	9.56**	8.05	3.20**	6.08
Pseudo R²	0.18		0.24		0.16		0.12	
N	5,039		5,039		5,039		5,039	

Note. *Significant at $p < .05$; ** significant at $p < .01$.
Source: ASPA Employers Survey (2009).

and productivity by means of demotion. They do, however, apply early retirement schemes more often, as well as accommodative measures like reduction of workload. With respect to the latter there may be a causality problem: employers who implement measures to reduce the workload may be perceiving a larger gap.

The results show sector differences. In industries and construction employers implement fewer training plans and more early retirement schemes than in the public sector. In addition, the services and trade sector is more involved in policies such as demotion and less in the reduction of workload than the public sector. The results also point at the importance of the size of organisations, as the existence of a policy for older workers is positively related to size. It may be that larger organisations have more opportunities to pursue policies and benefit more from economies of scale, as is the case with the implementation of training plans. High-skilled organisations implement more training plans. Organisations with a large share of older workers are more inclined to opt for early retirement schemes as well as for training plans and policies aimed at a reduction of workload. This last result suggests that the ageing of the workforce stimulates organisations to develop personnel policies in this area.

4.4.4.   Governmental policies
In the past, European institutions and national governments have been the main drivers in creating awareness about the necessity to extend working lives and set targets on the labour force participation of seniors (European Commission, 2002, 2006). With these earlier initiatives in mind, we presented employers with a list of possible measures governments can take to promote older workers' employment. We asked employers whether they considered these measures potentially effective or ineffective in improving older workers' labour force participation. Their answers are summarized in *table 4.6.*

Almost three-quarters of employers —up to 92 per cent in Denmark— favoured measures that allow for some kind of part-time retirement or bridge employment. Such measures may help older workers to carry on, even though they may no longer be as healthy or productive as they used to be. If older workers can retire on a part-time basis, employers will not have to pay any longer for all or part of non-productive hours or days. In France and Italy the expectations regarding the effectiveness of incentives to combine work and retirement are somewhat lower; this probably has to do with the fact that in those countries the combination of work and

Table 4.6. Governmental measures to retain older workers, percentage 'effective' and 'very effective'

	Pooled	Denmark	France	Germany	Italy	Netherlands	Poland	Sweden	UK
Incentives to combine work–retirement	74	92	55	80	63	78	69	68	-
Promoting lifelong learning	62	62	74	79	83	34	51	59	-
Wage subsidies for older workers	58	64	45	68	36	71	67	58	-
Lowering early retirement benefits	43	62	39	37	58	39	35	28	-
Laws preventing age discrimination	36	36	34	17	61	32	48	27	-
Media campaigns combating negative stereotypes	35	36	28	32	62	27	28	29	-

Source: ASPA Employers Survey (2009).

retirement is regulated by law — it was forbidden in France until 2003. The second measure is the promotion of lifelong learning, which may enhance productivity; this measure is considered most effective in Italy. This is remarkable, since Italian employers hardly indicated having some kind of training plan for older workers. On the other hand, maybe employers think they cannot or should not be responsible for lifelong learning, and therefore believe the government has to take responsibility for this. The third most effective measure according to employers are wage subsidies for older workers, which may 'compensate' organisations; this measure is considered especially effective in the Netherlands, Germany and Poland. Relatively often, in Italy employers consider laws preventing age discrimination and the combat against negative stereotypes to be effective measures. In the Netherlands and the UK such legislation already exists.

In *table 4.7* we present the results of a multivariate analysis carried out to examine the perceived effectiveness of governmental policies. We looked at three types of governmental policies related to lessening the wage-productivity gap by either reducing costs or increasing productivity:

1. Incentives to combine work and retirement (to balance productivity and costs);
2. Promotion of lifelong learning (to keep up labour productivity); and
3. Wage subsidies for older workers (to reduce costs).

We tested whether the perceived effectiveness of those measures is related to the expected wage-productivity gap. In the model we included country dummy variables as well as structural characteristics of the organisation, such as sector, age structure, skills level and size as control variables. The table shows that the expected wage-productivity gap is positively related to the perceived effectiveness of wage subsidies for older workers. Employers expecting an increasing wage-productivity gap are not more prone to consider the combination of work and retirement or the promotion of lifelong learning to be an effective governmental policy.

The results show some sector differences. In industries and construction, employers consider all three governmental policies less effective than in the public sector; in services and trade the promotion of lifelong learning is considered less effective than in the public sector. With respect to size, the results show that large organisations consider the promotion of lifelong learning to be an effective policy more often than small organisations, while wage subsidies are perceived to be an effective measure especially

Table 4.7. Perceived effectiveness governmental policies (ordered logistic regression analysis)

	Combine work-retirement		Promote lifelong learning		Wage subsidies for older workers	
	Odds ratio	Z-value	Odds ratio	Z-value	Odds ratio	Z-value
Expected wage-productivity gap	1.06	1.60	0.95	-1.30	1.10**	2.58
Sector of industry (public sector = reference category)						
* Industries and construction	0.83*	-2.46	0.72**	-4.35	0.86*	-2.09
* Services and trade	0.91	-1.19	0.81**	-2.75	0.94	-0.86
Size of the organisation (logarithm)	1.02	0.92	1.19**	8.98	0.91**	-5.12
Skill level of workers						
Share of employees in high-skilled jobs	1.03	0.30	1.51**	3.69	0.85	-1.44
Share of employees in unskilled jobs	0.97	-0.27	0.67**	-3.50	1.03	0.25
Share of older workers	1.02	0.11	0.87	-0.83	0.75	-1.67
Countries (Sweden = reference category)						
Denmark	3.40**	9.62	1.51**	3.35	1.49**	3.31
Germany	1.41**	2.89	3.02**	9.26	1.23	1.80
Italy	0.53**	-5.31	3.26**	9.86	0.32**	-9.78
Netherlands	1.73**	4.69	0.63**	-4.08	2.00**	6.20
Poland	0.91	-0.86	0.80*	-1.97	1.81**	5.37
Pseudo R^2	0.04		0.06		0.04	
N	4,525		4,525		4,525	

Note. *Significant at $p < .05$; ** significant at $p < .01$.
Source: ASPA Employers Survey (2009).

by smaller organisations. The perceived effectiveness of the promotion of lifelong learning is positively related to the share of high-skilled workers in an organisation.

4.5. Conclusion and discussion

This study addressed four main questions: Do European employers take action to extend working lives in terms of recruitment and retention of older workers? What do employers see as possible consequences of an ageing workforce for their own organisation? What organisational policies do European employers apply to retain older workers? And —according to employers— what can governments do to extend working lives?

Both recruitment and retention levels of older workers are rather low in all of the countries included in this study, and employers' actions to extend working lives have a stronger focus on retention than on recruitment of older workers. There also seems to be a normative barrier in employers' behaviour: recruitment and retention beyond the statutory age of retirement is not applied by many employers. Our results show important outcomes with respect to perceived changes in costs and benefits as the workforce ages, as a substantial number of employers foresee an increasing wage-productivity gap. This perceived gap may explain employers' reluctance to hire and stimulate older workers to continue working until or even beyond the existing retirement age.

So far, organisational policies do not seem to be aimed at tackling the wage-productivity gap. Although demotion and lifelong learning are suggested by scientists and policy makers as a way to bridge the gap between labour costs and productivity, the enthusiasm for actual implementation of these measures is not shared by employers. Except for the UK, employers do not apply demotion of older workers to balance pay and productivity. Also, additional training to prevent or counter a decline in productivity is given by only a minority of employers. Demotion and training are not implemented more often by employers expecting a larger wage-productivity gap. On the contrary, early retirement schemes and reduction of workload without remuneration adjustments are applied more often by employers expecting a larger pay-productivity gap.

Our study is among the first to address employers' views on governmental policies concerning older workers and extending working life. The most effective governmental measure to increase labour force participation of older workers —according to employers— are incentives to combine work and retirement. A preference for such a combination suggests there is room for older workers to extend their working lives inside organisations, albeit in an adjusted form. Phased retirement is one way to combine work and retirement, and may also include —in the wording of the TLM approach (Klosse and Schippers, 2008)— preventive transitions. Preventive transitions are a form of career mobility that prevents older workers from getting stuck in a job where they gradually lose their productivity. Another possibility is bridge employment. Bridge employment means that older workers work in any form between their career jobs and full retirement, for instance by taking a part-time job or other temporary employment prior to definitive retirement, within the same occupation or in the same position, or in a completely different job. In the literature bridge employment is described as becoming more common, and its occurrence is expected to further increase (Cahill *et al.*, 2006; Johnson *et al.*, 2009).

The second and third most effective governmental measures to increase labour force participation of older workers are the promotion of lifelong learning and wage subsidies. The larger the labour cost-productivity gap employers expect, the more often they consider wage subsidies to be an effective measure to increase the labour force participation of older workers. This suggests that employers expect governments to partly facilitate the process of bridging the gap between pay and productivity. Interestingly, the effectiveness of wage subsidies is rated high by employers in small organisations, which are much less involved in policy initiatives to improve the productivity of older workers and may be more dependent on government support.

Our study shows that although policy makers have put great efforts into the promotion of older workers' labour participation, relatively few employers are behaving in a way that actively supports a trend towards working longer. The international comparison shows that the lack of action from employers to activate senior potential is not a matter of just one specific country. This does not imply that European employers show a uniform pattern in their attitudes and behaviour towards older workers: outcomes do not follow a 'European way' and are not distinguishable by type of welfare state, and national contexts do turn out to be highly relevant. Attitudes and behaviour of Swedish employers, for example, differ considerably from those of their Danish colleagues (both belonging to Esping-Andersen's, 1990 social-democratic welfare state), and equally large variation exists between German and French employers (both belonging to the continental/conservative welfare state type). Any solutions along the lines of 'one European way' of stimulating extension of working lives and increasing labour force participation of older workers therefore seem to be —at least at this point in time— not necessarily viable. The results are not distinguishable by economic climate either. In earlier research, Conen *et al.* (2011) showed for the Netherlands that changes in the demand for workers affect employers' recruitment and retention behaviour towards older workers. Although unemployment rates vary highly between the countries under study, we do not find a divide between employers showing more activating behaviour towards their older workers in countries with low unemployment rates than in countries with high unemployment rates.

There are several noteworthy contributions of this study to the existing literature. First, the study addresses employers' perspective on the extension of working lives, a perspective that is often neglected when compared to research on attitudes and behaviour of older workers themselves and to research on institutional arrangements affecting both supply of and demand for older workers. Another contribution of the study is that it is among the first to report on employers' policies and practices from countries from all parts of Europe and from all types of European welfare states. The cross-national dimension is important, as it provides information on whether employers' attitudes and actions towards older workers are either a national phenomenon or can be more widely found among European employers.

The study does have a number of limitations. One limitation is that, although the dataset is sizeable, it is difficult to assess to what extent the national samples are representative of the population of interest due to the varying response rates. A low response rate can give rise to sampling bias if the non-response is unequally distributed. However, there is no minimum for an 'acceptable' response rate: research suggests that in many cases surveys with varying response rates yield results that are statistically indistinguishable (Keeter *et al.*, 2006). Another limitation is its reliance on self-reported behaviour. Respondents may be reporting that they recruit or retain older workers or apply policies in accordance with a dominant organisational or national policy even though they are not really complying. Future studies may combine self-reported behaviour with direct measures of hiring and retention behaviour.

In this survey we found European employers to be little involved in extending older workers' careers, and the dominant consequence of the ageing of the workforce is perceived to be a growing gap between labour costs and productivity. A logical next question is whether these perceived consequences are accurate, or whether employers underestimate or overestimate the development of labour costs and productivity as the workforce ages. Future researchers may want to combine employers' perceptions about developments in labour costs and productivity and actual measures within organisations.

5. Ageing and employers' perceptions of labour costs and productivity: a survey among European employers[1]

Abstract

This study examines employers' perceptions of changes in the labour cost-productivity gap due to the ageing of the workforce, the effects of tenure wages and employment protection on the perceived gap, and whether a perceived labour cost-productivity gap affects employers' recruitment and retention behaviour towards older workers. We analyse surveys administered to employers in Denmark, France, Germany, Italy, the Netherlands, Poland and Sweden. The results show that approximately half of employers associate the ageing of the personnel with a growing gap between labour costs and productivity. Both the presence of tenure wages and employment protection rules increase the probability of employers perceiving a widening labour cost-productivity gap due to the ageing of their workforce. A counterfactual shows that even when employment protection and tenure wage systems are abolished, 40 per cent of employers expect a net cost increase. The expected labour cost-productivity gap negatively affects both recruitment and retention of older workers.

5.1. Introduction

Employers play a key role in older workers' labour mobility and possibilities to retain their jobs. Barriers for employers to hire or retain older workers are often attributed to an increasing wage-productivity gap. For instance, the OECD (2006) states "To the extent that labour costs of older workers rise faster than their productivity, employers may be reluctant to either retain workers beyond a certain age or hire older workers" (p. 67). In this study we examine the perceived consequences of an ageing staff on labour costs and productivity, and whether such perceptions are related to employers' behaviour towards older workers.

Various methods have been used to examine the relationship between age, wages and productivity. Many studies use matched worker-firm datasets

---

[1] This chapter was published earlier as Conen W.S., K. Henkens and J.J. Schippers, 2012, Ageing and employers' perceptions of labour costs and productivity: A survey among European employers. *International Journal of Manpower*, 33(6), 629-647. Reprinted with permission from Emerald Group Publishing Limited.

linking age-earnings profiles to plant-level production functions based on either cross-sectional information (*e.g.* Hellerstein and Neumark, 2004) or panel data (*cf.* Crépon *et al.*, 2002; Van Ours and Stoeldraijer, 2011).

Empirical evidence on the relationship between age, wages and productivity is inconclusive. Some studies find workers' wage-productivity gap to increase with age (Kotlikoff and Gokhale, 1992; Flabbi and Ichino, 2001; Crépon *et al.*, 2002; Hellerstein and Neumark, 2004; Ilmakunnas and Maliranta, 2005), while others find little evidence of such a gap (Aubert and Crépon, 2007; Van Ours and Stoeldraijer, 2011). The cited articles predominantly try to establish a relationship between the age structure of the workforce and 'objective' measures of labour productivity and costs.

We approach the wage-productivity gap from a different perspective by examining the perceptions of employers using a survey. The central research questions of this study are the following: First, what are the determinants of the perceived changes in the labour cost-productivity gap due to the ageing of the workforce? Second, to what extent does this perceived gap affect employers' recruitment and retention of older workers?

In answering our first research question we focus on two factors that are assumed to hamper or stifle flexibility in the labour market: tenure wages and employment protection. Tenure wages are wages that rise with tenure, apart from the employee's formal qualifications and performance within the organisation. Organisations with a steep tenure-wage profile are more likely to be confronted with a labour cost-productivity gap in the face of an ageing personnel structure. In our study, employment protection refers to the perceived difficulty of firing a worker with a permanent contract. Employment protection regulations have been at the centre of heated policy debate in Europe (Siebert, 1997; Blanchard, 2004). The central issue in offering employment protection is to strike a balance between the interests of employers (flexibility for organisations) and those of employees (job security). From the employers' perspective, employment protection may hold both costs and benefits for employers. With respect to costs, employment protection can diminish the ability to cope with a changing environment. Employment protection may also strengthen wage bargaining positions of 'insiders' (OECD, 2004; Addison and Teixeira, 2003). But protection may also have benefits for both employers and employees: long-term contracts create an environment that may enhance productivity by encouraging human capital accumulation (*cf.* Belot *et al.*, 2002). Whether employment protection regulation is a boon or a bane remains an unresolved issue. This study addresses the question of whether organisations experiencing high levels of employment protection have different expectations regarding a labour cost-productivity gap than those organisations facing low protection levels.

Our second research question focuses on whether a perceived gap between labour costs and productivity affects employers' recruitment and retention behaviour towards older workers. Although there is no general consensus about the link between age, wages and productivity, the evidence seems to be unambiguous with respect to the vulnerability of older workers in the labour market. Early retirement tends to be a one-way street and older workers' opportunities to re-enter the labour force after a period of unemployment or to change jobs at the end of a working life are limited and largely determined by employers (OECD, 2006; Berger, 2009). It is suggested that negative perceptions about labour costs and productivity of older workers are critical barriers to their employment prospects (OECD, 2006).

We collected data among European employers and asked about their attitudes towards older workers and retention and hiring behaviour. The cross-national dimension provides information on whether employers' perceptions vary per country or are a more European-wide characteristic among employers. The data come from surveys conducted in Denmark, France, Germany, Italy, the Netherlands, Poland and Sweden in 2009. Employers from the various countries face different labour market situations and institutional arrangements affecting both supply of and demand for older workers. The pooling of these diverse experiences provides more robust and clearer perspectives on how ageing and labour market institutions affect employers' views and behaviour.

The next section addresses the theoretical background of the relationship between ageing, labour costs and productivity. Section 3 presents the data and variables of interest. The results are presented in section 4 and in section 5 we conclude with a summary of the main findings and discussion.

5.2.   Ageing, labour costs and productivity

Several strands of economic theory provide a basis for hypotheses examining the link between age, labour costs and labour productivity. The first strand is the spot market theory which states that in a perfectly competitive labour market firms pay workers according to their marginal product, regardless of the age of the worker. In spot market theory an age-related wage-productivity gap would not occur by definition. As productivity is often difficult or costly to assess, in most organisations it is not a viable option for employers to pay workers according to their marginal productivity.

The second strand of economic theory comes from human capital theory (Becker, 1962; for an overview, see Polachek and Siebert, 1993). The theory states that investments in human capital boost labour productivity, and productivity is positively related to remuneration of employees. In principle, people accumulate human capital through training and experience during the whole of their career, but most investments in training take place at younger ages. Human capital also may depreciate, *e.g.* because knowledge of older technologies becomes obsolete or because cognitive and physical skills deteriorate. Depreciation of human capital will lead to a decrease in productivity.

In the late 1970s, the relationship between age, labour costs and productivity as described by human capital theory was called into question (Hutchens, 1989), giving rise to different kinds of contract theories, such as Lazear's (1979) delayed payment contract theory. This theory states that employers may have implicit contracts with their employees regarding the connection between productivity and income over their career: while earnings are lower than productivity during the first phase of a worker's career, earnings are higher than productivity during the second phase. Such contracts induce employees to perform at a higher level of effort and reduce workers incentives to shirk. A different type of contract theory, such as that of Harris and Holmstrom (1982), takes into account the uncertainty about the productivity of newly recruited workers, which translates into offering them relatively low wages. Another variation on the theme takes into account worker reliability. Since younger workers by definition cannot have a reputation for reliability, they pay a higher wage premium, thus effectively receiving lower wage offers (Grossman, 1977). All these contract theories imply a present value relationship between compensation and productivity, boiling down to a distribution in which younger workers' productivity exceed wages and older workers' wages exceed productivity.

As Lazear (1979) argues, incentive theories are consistent with mandatory retirement. He stresses that "A necessary consequence of this payment schedule is mandatory retirement, that is, a date at which the contract is terminated and the worker is no longer entitled to receive a wage greater than his VMP [value of the worker's marginal product]" (Lazear, 1979, p. 1283). Employers will therefore either opt for mandatory retirement schedules or for the use of private pension schemes that penalise continued employment beyond a certain age. An additional complication with contract models, with their relatively high remuneration for older workers, is that the sustainability of the contracts is negatively affected by the ageing of the workforce. An increase in the number of older —and relatively highly paid— workers reduces the financial sustainability of an organisation and increases incentives for organisations to either decrease wages of older workers, renegotiate the promise to retain the workers until the mandatory retirement age or lay them off.

An element that might affect employers' decisions is the level of employment protection. Strong employment protection rules may weaken the adaptability of organisations to alleviate the possible negative consequences of an ageing workforce. Contrary to a host of macro-economic research that focuses on the *de jure* level of employment protection as measured by the OECD, this study uses the level of employment protection as perceived by individual employers. There is some evidence as to why perceptions of regulations may be of importance in understanding actual decisions. For instance, Boeri and Jimeno (2005) show that small firms are often exempted from certain aspects of labour regulations, or do not comply when enforcement is weak. In general, one would expect de jure regulations to impact labour demand; research by Pierre and Scarpetta (2006), who employ the World Bank's Investment Climate Survey, shows that firms in developing countries facing stricter employment legislation are more likely to report regulations being a major obstacle to their operation. However, they also show that larger firms and innovating firms tend to be more sensitive to the strictness of regulations. In short, it matters to pay special attention to the individual circumstances in which firms operate, and under those circumstances perceptions of the strictness of regulations may even offer a better approximation of the way rules and regulations function in a country. Employers face uncertainty about future developments in labour costs and productivity of individual employees, and this uncertainty plays a large role in hiring decisions. Although diplomas, job interviews and references may provide an idea of the abilities of new personnel, how productive they will be remains to be seen. Employers have access to what Phelps (1972) has called 'previous statistical experience': information on how certain categories or groups of employees tend to behave and develop. This experience affects their hiring decision, and as formalised by Thurow (1975) it determines to a large extent the place of job candidates in the job queue. The 'job queue' represents the idea of employers —who are in the process of recruitment and selection— ranking potential employees and placing them in a fictitious order of preference. Employers select the candidates in turn, until their demand for labour has been met. If employers associate seniority with a larger labour cost-productivity gap, it will presumably negatively affect the relative position of older workers in this 'job queue'.

This short overview of the theory on the relationship between age, labour costs and productivity can be formalised into three specific hypotheses which will be the focus of this study:

1. Tenure wage hypothesis. Organisations that apply tenure-based wage profiles are more likely to expect an increasing labour cost-productivity gap due to ageing of the workforce than organisations without such seniority wage rules.
2. Employment protection hypothesis. Employers who perceive the level of employment protection to be high are more likely to perceive a larger labour cost-productivity gap due to an ageing of the workforce than those employers who perceive this level of protection to be low.
3. Recruitment and retention hypothesis. The perception of a larger labour cost-productivity gap negatively influences employers' retention and hiring behaviour towards older workers.

5.3. Methodology

5.3.1.   Survey among employers

Data on employers' behaviour and attitudes were collected between March and November 2009. The countries included in this study are geographically dispersed over Europe and cover all types of European welfare state regimes. Sweden and Denmark represent Esping-Andersen's (1990) social-democratic welfare state, the UK stands for the liberal welfare state, and the Netherlands, Germany and France stand for the continental/conservative welfare state. As several authors (Leibfried, 1992; Ferrera, 1996; Bonoli, 1997) also distinguish a fourth category, the Mediterranean type of welfare state, we also included Italy. Finally, Poland represents a 'new' —former eastern European— European Union (EU) member state. We used data from comparative surveys carried out among employers in Denmark, France, Germany, Italy, the Netherlands, Poland and Sweden[2].

---

[2]   Data from the UK was left out because a shorter questionnaire was used that did not cover the questions on seniority wage and recruitment and retention behaviour, some of the main themes in this study.

The total number of completed questionnaires amounts to 5,822, of which 609 are from Denmark, 500 from France, 892 from Germany, 770 from Italy, 1,077 from the Netherlands, 1,037 from Poland and 525 from Sweden. The overall response rate was 23 per cent and ranged from 7 to 53 per cent for the different countries. This is lower than the average response rate for individual surveys but in line with the rate generally found in corporate surveys. In Europe and the USA, response rates have been found to be 20-30 per cent at most (see Brewster *et al.*, 1994; Kalleberg *et al.*, 1996; Van Dalen *et al.*, 2009).

The questionnaires were completed by directors / chief executive officers [CEOs] / chief financial officers [CFOs] (29%), heads of departments and general managers (16%) and human resource managers (33%); this 'higher management' group adds up to at least 79 per cent, and is likely to be well informed and have good insight into the policies and practices of the organisation. A total of 61 per cent of respondents reported that an academic degree was required for their job. The average age of respondents was 46 and 50 per cent of respondents were male.

The questionnaires used in the different countries were identical. Interview techniques used differed between countries, depending on what was perceived to be the best way to address respondents in a specific country. Denmark used computer-assisted web interviewing; Germany, the Netherlands and Sweden used paper and pencil interviewing; and France, Italy and Poland used computer-assisted telephone interviewing.

For all countries we drew a stratified sample on the characteristics of establishments' sector and size. In the analyses at the national level we weighted the data afterwards to account for the sampling design, to ensure the observations were representative for the population of employers. Weights are constructed according to the population of establishments from national statistics bureaus and corrected for establishment sector and size. To present results at the pooled level, we pooled the data for all seven countries —including the national weighting factors— and constructed a new weighting factor that takes the net sample size of the different countries into account. Otherwise, Dutch and Polish employers (N>1,000) would influence results more than French and Swedish employers (N≈500).

5.3.2.   Measures

Dependent variables.
Perceptions of a labour cost-productivity gap[3] were based on the following two questions: 'What would the consequences in your organization be if the average age of your personnel increased by five years?' Response items included labour costs and labour productivity (answer categories: '1' strong decline, '2' decline, '3' stays the same, '4' increase, '5' strong increase). The combination of the expectations on labour costs and productivity translate into expectations on the development of the labour cost-productivity gap with an ageing workforce. For instance, when an employer expects productivity to stay the same but labour costs to increase, this implies an increase of the labour cost-productivity gap. A scale of the expected labour cost-productivity gap was constructed by grouping together respondents who expect the gap to decrease (-1), stay the same (0) or increase (1). In *table 5.1* the relevant scores are presented for the different combinations of changes in labour costs and productivity.

Retention behaviour was operationalised by asking respondents whether they encouraged workers to continue working until they reach age 65 ('1' currently applied, '0' not applied). Recruitment behaviour was operationalised by asking whether employers recruited older workers ('1' currently applied, '0' not applied). 'Older workers' were defined in the questionnaire as 'workers ages 50 years or older'. Descriptive statistics of the variables used in the analyses are presented in *table 5.2.*

Independent variables.
Tenure wage. Tenure wage was measured by the question 'To what extent, apart from the employee's formal qualifications and his function in the organisation, do wages rise with tenure (*i.e.* the number of years that the employee has worked in your organisation)?' (answering categories: '1' not at all to '4' to a high extent). Tenure wages are usually implemented by using salary scales, which automatically increase by one step each year.

Employment protection. Employment protection legislation generally refers to the entire set of regulations affecting both hiring and firing policies. We focus on protection of permanent workers against individual dismissal,

---

[3] Labour costs may consist of both direct wages and additional labour costs (such as extra leave or sickness absenteeism). Although 'wages' and 'labour costs' are not the same, in the economic literature it is more common to talk about a wage-productivity gap than about a labour cost-productivity gap. We therefore use 'wages' and 'labour costs' interchangeably.

Table 5.1. Relevant groups in the analyses of a labour cost-productivity gap as a result of an ageing personnel structure

		Labour costs		
		Decrease	Stable	Increase
	Decrease	0	1	1
Productivity	Stable	-1	0	1
	Increase	-1	-1	0

which is highly relevant in terms of organisations' adaptability to alleviate the possible negative consequences of an ageing workforce. This measure is based on the question: 'How difficult is it in your organisation to fire a worker with a permanent contract?' (answering categories: '1' very easy to '5' very difficult). Our measure captures perceived employment protection at the organisational level rather than objective measures of legislation at the national level, as performed for instance by OECD[4]. This different stance towards employment protection is complementary in the sense that perceptions may differ between employers within a country: the perceived level of employment protection needs not be grounded in law, but can also originate from collective bargaining of social partners, organisational culture and individual characteristics or experiences of employers.

Control variables.
In the analyses we controlled for sector of industry, organizational features and country. To control for sector differences, respondents were given a list of industrial sectors defined by Eurostat (2002) and were asked to indicate the sector in which their own organisation operated. We categorised the sectors into 'industries', 'construction', 'services and trade', 'public sector' and 'education, health and social work'. The control variables on organisational characteristics were assessed using five variables. Respondents were asked for the total number of employees in their organisation (size), share of high-skilled workers, share of workers with fixed-term temporary contracts and share of older workers; these are all continuous variables. The extent of absenteeism/sickness rate was based on the question 'To what extent

---

[4]   We note that the OECD (2010b) distinguishes three pillars of employment protection legislation: First, protection of permanent workers against individual dismissal; Second, specific requirements for collective dismissal; Third, regulation for temporary forms of employments. Our questionnaire captures primarily the perception of the strictness of the first pillar. In our study the effects of employment protection on the labour cost-productivity gap might therefore be an underestimation, as we did not include all aspects of employment protection.

Table 5.2. Descriptive statistics

	Mean	SD	Min	Max
Dependent variables				
Expected labour cost-productivity gap (-1 = decline, 1 = increase)	0.53	0.60	-1	1
Recruitment of older workers (0=no, 1=yes)	0.14	0.35	0	1
Retention of older workers (0=no, 1=yes)	0.26	0.44	0	1
Independent variables				
Tenure wages (1 = none, 4 = highly applicable)	2.57	0.78	1	4
Difficulty of dismissing a worker (1 = very easy, 5 = very difficult)	3.81	0.96	1	5
Control variables				
Sector of industry (Industries = reference category)				
Construction	0.09	0.28	0	1
Services and trade	0.32	0.47	0	1
Public sector	0.12	0.33	0	1
Education, health care and social work	0.21	0.41	0	1
Size (logarithm)	4.46	1.52	0	13.12
Share of high-skilled workers	0.26	0.29	0	1
Share of workers with fixed-term temporary contract	0.11	0.18	0	1
Share of older workers	0.25	0.17	0	1
Extent of absenteeism/ sickness rate	1.43	0.62	1	3

Experienced shortages (no shortages = reference category)				
Some vacancies	0.36	0.48	0	1
Many vacancies	0.79	0.27	0	1
Countries (Denmark = reference category)				
France	0.05	0.21	0	1
Germany	0.16	0.37	0	1
Italy	0.14	0.35	0	1
Netherlands	0.19	0.40	0	1
Poland	0.18	0.39	0	1
Sweden	0.09	0.29	0	1

does your establishment encounter any of the following problems related to personnel: High absenteeism and/or high sickness rate?' (answering categories: '1' no/to a low extent to '3' to a high extent). Since the number of countries is too small to perform multilevel analyses to test for macro-level effects (*cf.* Maas and Hox, 2005), we controlled for country characteristics by including country dummies.

5.3.3.   Analyses

We used ordered logistic regression models to estimate the impact of tenure wages, employment protection and control variables on the perceived labour cost-productivity gap. In these models the outcome variable was treated as ordinal, as the response levels have a natural ranking (decline, no change, increase) despite our not knowing the actual distances between contiguous levels. Nonetheless, for the results of such models to be valid they must meet the criteria for proportional odds. Since the ordered logit model estimates one equation over all levels of the dependent variable (as compared to the multinomial logit model), the test for proportional odds tests the validity of our one-equation model. We used a χ^2-test for proportional odds. The results suggest that the assumption of proportional odds was not violated. We therefore analysed the data using ordered logistic regression analyses in which the values of our dependent variable are treated as ordinal variables. To examine to what extent the perceived gap affects employers' recruitment and retention of older workers, we performed multivariate logistic regression.

5.4.   Results

5.4.1.   Perceptions of changes in labour cost-productivity gap

We addressed the question of whether organisations expect changes in the labour cost-productivity gap due to an ageing workforce. *Table 5.3* shows to what extent employers expect an ageing workforce to affect labour costs and productivity within their organisation. The first part of the table presents the expectations regarding the influence of ageing on labour costs. For the pooled sample we show that almost half of employers expect an increase in labour costs. There are, however, large differences between countries. In Poland and Denmark up to one-third of employers expect labour costs to increase. In Sweden, Germany, Italy and France roughly half of employers expect costs to increase. Employers in the Netherlands are at the other end of the spectrum: here 75 per cent think labour costs will increase due to an ageing workforce. Only very few employers expect a decline of labour costs. The latter finding is in accordance with insights from OECD (2006)

Table 5.3. European employers' perceptions of the consequences of an ageing personnel structure of own organisation (%)

Consequences	Pooled	Denmark	France	Germany	Italy	Netherlands	Poland	Sweden
Labour costs								
Increase	44	33	51	48	49	75	16	44
Same	52	61	43	51	48	24	74	50
Decline	4	6	6	1	3	1	10	6
Labour productivity								
Increase	10	10	7	10	14	8	10	8
Same	62	71	64	54	62	58	61	55
Decline	28	19	28	36	25	34	29	37
Cost-productivity gap[b]								
Increase	53	41	55	61	50	75	31	59
Same	41	51	38	36	45	23	58	35
Decline	6	8	7	3	5	2	11	6

Notes: [a] Based on the question: 'If the average age of your personnel increases by five years, what will be the effect on[...]?'
[b] Based on cross-tabulating expected consequences in labour costs and labour productivity.
Source: ASPA Employers Survey (2009).

based on cross-sectional macro-data and Deelen (2011), who shows for a large administrative database that wage-tenure profiles in the Netherlands are steep.

With respect to the connection between ageing and productivity, the results show that in all countries a majority of employers state that productivity as such is not affected by the ageing of the workforce. However, a substantial minority (28%) expects productivity to decrease (strongly); this is the highest in Sweden, where 37 per cent of employers expect a productivity decline and the lowest in Denmark (19%).

The combination of the expectations on labour costs and productivity translate into expectations on the development of the labour cost-productivity gap with an ageing workforce, which is shown in the third part of the table. We combined the answers on changes in labour costs and labour productivity to establish whether employers perceive a net cost or a net productivity increase as a result of an ageing workforce. Overall, about half of employers expect an ageing workforce to be associated with a net labour cost increase (53%). The table shows large differences between countries. Dutch employers are most sceptical when it comes to expectations about the consequences of an ageing staff: 75 per cent of employers expect a net labour cost increase as the workforce ages, and only 2 per cent expect a decline. In Poland the wage-productivity gap is less of an issue; in this country about one-third of employers expect a net cost increase and 11 per cent expect a net productivity increase.

5.4.2.   Tenure wages and employment protection
In this section we examine tenure wages and employment protection rules as possible underlying predictors of an expected labour cost-productivity gap. *Figure 5.1* shows that 58 per cent of employers report wages to rise with tenure to 'a high' or 'some' extent in their own organisation. Automatic increases in salary scales are mostly observed among Dutch and French organisations (78 and 72%, respectively). In Germany, only 36 per cent of employers indicate that wages rise with tenure in their own organisation. These results on tenure wages correspond largely to those found by the OECD (1998; 2006; 2010a).

Figure 5.2 shows that 56 per cent of employers indicate it is 'difficult/very difficult' to fire a worker with a permanent contract. In Italy, the Netherlands, Sweden, Germany and France a majority of employers perceive a high level of employment protection. In Denmark, only 25 per cent of employers report

Figure 5.1. European employers' perception of wages rising with tenure

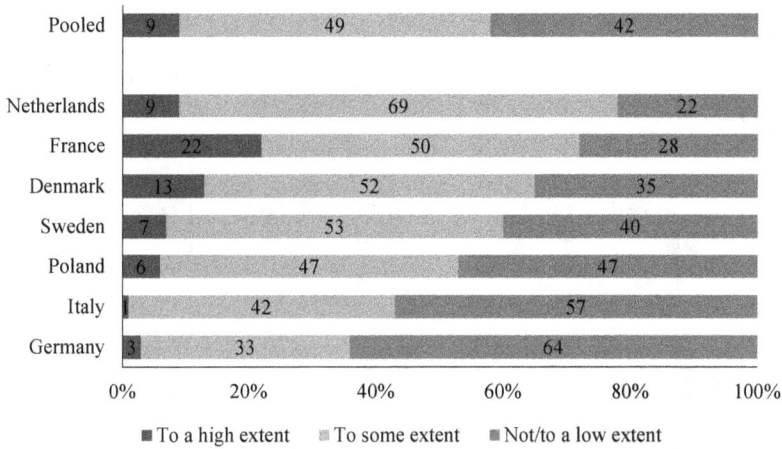

Note: Based on the question: To what extent, apart from the employee's formal qualifications and
his function in the organisation, do wages rise with tenure (*i.e.* the number of years that the
employee has worked in your establishment)?

Source: ASPA Employers Survey (2009).

Figure 5.2. European employers' perception of level of employment
protection

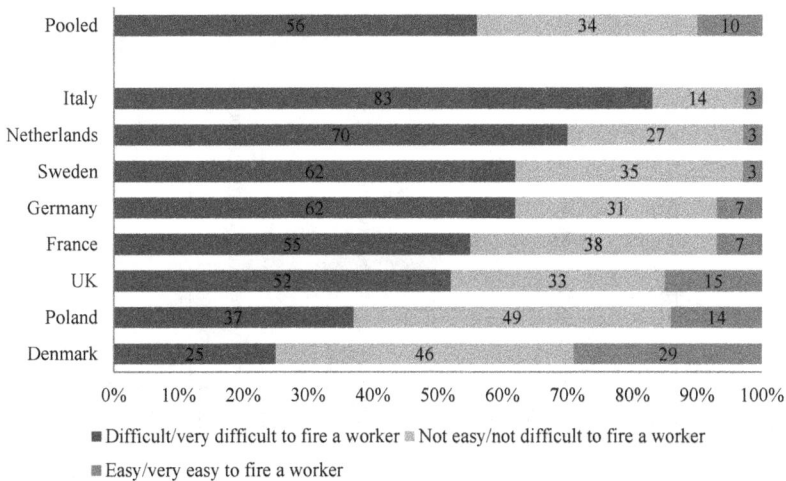

Note: Based on the question: How difficult is it in your establishment to fire a worker with a
permanent contract?

Source: ASPA Employers Survey (2009).

Table 5.4. Explaining expected labour cost-productivity gap (ordered logistic regression analysis)

	GAP[a]			
	Model 1		Model 2	
	Odds ratio	z-value	Odds ratio	z-value
Wage				
Tenure wage	-	-	1.18**	4.29
Employment protection				
Difficulty of dismissing a worker	-	-	1.13**	3.40
Control variables				
Sector of industry (industries = reference category):				
Construction	0.83	-1.56	0.84	-1.46
Services and trade	0.87	-1.72	0.85*	-2.00
Public sector	1.20	1.74	1.09	0.77
Education, health care and social work	1.32**	2.90	1.22*	2.03
Organisational features:				
Size (logarithm)	1.11**	4.74	1.10**	4.42
Share of high-skilled workers	1.03	0.30	1.00	0.03
Share of workers with fixed-term temporary contract	0.73	-1.76	0.76	-1.55
Share of older workers	1.58*	2.54	1.59*	2.57

Extent of absenteeism/ sickness rate	1.29**	4.95	1.26**	4.50
Countries (Denmark = reference category):				
France	2.42**	6.76	2.11**	5.57
Germany	2.96***	9.94	2.79***	8.79
Italy	1.61***	4.62	1.43**	3.03
Netherlands	5.90**	15.06	5.11**	13.31
Poland	0.83	-1.74	0.82	-1.80
Sweden	2.00**	6.54	1.85**	5.53
Pseudo R^2	0.07		0.08	
N	4,947		4,947	

*Significant at $p < .05$; ** significant at $p < .01$.

[a] The scale of the expected labour cost-productivity gap ranges from -1 to 1 and was based on cross-tabulating expected consequences in labour costs and labour productivity.

Source: ASPA Employers Survey (2009).

finding it difficult to dismiss a worker, which is in line with the Danish 'flexicurity' model. The high perceived level of employment protection in Italy is interesting, because according to OECD (2010b) protection of permanent workers against dismissal is relatively low in Italy.

The next step is to test our hypotheses about the two possible factors influencing the labour cost-productivity gap: tenure wages and employment protection rules. The first model of *table 5.4* presents results from the ordered logistic regression analysis explaining the labour cost-productivity gap by control variables only: organisational features, sector of industry and country. In the second model we added seniority wages and employment protection.

The estimation results show that the steepness of the tenure-wage profile is positively related to the perceived change in the labour cost-productivity gap[5]. In other words, in organisations where wages rise to a higher extent with tenure employers are more likely to expect a net cost increase due to an ageing staff. Regarding employment protection, the results show that employers who perceive the level of employment protection to be high are more likely to expect a net labour cost increase.

In the literature it is sometimes suggested to include a bargaining structure variable (*cf.* Addison and Teixeira, 2003), since there is a potential omitted variables problem if unionisation is correlated with employment protection and/or tenure wages. We tested whether this is the case in our model by adding the variable approximating the labour union power. This variable is based on the question: 'The influence of labour unions on personnel policies is clearly visible in this organisation' ('1' completely disagree, '5' completely agree) (not in table). Adding this variable did not alter our results.

The results show that compared to the reference group (industries), organisations in 'services and trade' are less likely to perceive a net cost increase, whereas organisations in 'education, health care and social work' have more frequent expectations of such a gap occurring. Employers who already have a larger proportion of older workers in their staff or who encounter high absenteeism problems are more likely to expect a net cost increase. Employers' perceptions vary across countries regarding the gap between labour costs and productivity due to ageing staff, as is shown in the lower part of table 5.4 National contexts may be particularly relevant when

---

[5]　Results of the separate estimation results for the analyses of perceived labour costs and productivity can be obtained from the authors upon request.

examining the effects of tenure wages and employment protection. There are significant interaction effects between country and tenure wage and between country and employment protection (see the *Appendix A.2*). Compared to European employers, for German employers tenure wages and employment protection are more positively related to an expected net cost increase. For Dutch employers, tenure wages are more related to the perceived gap and for Swedish employers employment protection is less related to the perceived gap. For all countries, the main effects remain significant after adding the two-way interactions.

To gain more insight into the effects of tenure wages and employment protection on the perceived labour cost-productivity gap, we performed a simple counterfactual analysis in which the application of tenure wages and the level of employment protection are varied. We calculated the predicted scores on the dependent variable based on the model in table 5.4, and examined a situation in which the tenure-wage profile is completely absent as well as one in which the perceived employment protection is reduced to a minimum level.

Table 5.5 shows that in the baseline case 53 per cent of employers expect a net cost increase as a result of an ageing workforce and only 6 per cent expect a net productivity increase. The central question of this exercise is, to what extent the share of employers who expect a change in the gap between costs and productivity is affected by these labour market reforms? In the extreme case of wages not rising with tenure and a low level of employment protection, 40 per cent of employers expect a net cost increase and 10 per cent expect a net productivity increase; the model thus shows a 13-percentage point decline compared to the baseline situation of a net cost increase and a 4-percentage point increase for a net productivity increase. In other words, although these types of labour market reforms have a substantial effect on the financial sustainability of organisations, they do not neutralise the expected consequences of an ageing workforce: 40 per cent of employers still expect a net cost increase as a result of an ageing workforce.

5.4.3. Recruitment and retention behaviour

Table 5.6 presents the logistic regression analysis of employers' recruitment and retention of employees as dependent variables. We test whether the perception of a labour cost-productivity gap is a predictor of employers' recruitment and retention behaviour towards older workers. The odds ratio represents the ratio of the probability of employers recruiting or retaining

Table 5.5. Results of a counterfactual analysis of the consequences of abolishing tenure-based wages and employment protection on an expected labour cost-productivity gap

	Share of employers expecting a labour cost-productivity gap		
	Net cost increase (Δcost > Δproductivity)	Stable (Δcost = Δproductivity)	Net productivity increase (Δcost < Δproductivity)
	%	%	%
Baseline model[a]	53	41	6
Wages do not increase with tenure[b]	48	44	8
Low level of employment protection[c]	46	46	8
Combined effects of 1 and 2[d]	40	50	10

Notes: [a] Baseline model is based on the estimation results of model 2 in table 5.3.

[b] In this counterfactual analysis the score for tenure wages is set to 1 (lower limit).

[c] In this counterfactual analysis the score for employment protection is set to 1 (lower limit).

[d] In this counterfactual analysis both the scores for tenure wages and employment protection are set to 1.

Source: ASPA Employers Survey (2009)

older workers compared to the probability of them not hiring or retaining older workers.

Column 1 of table 5.6 shows that employers who expect a net cost increase due to an ageing staff are significantly less likely to recruit older workers. In column 3 we see that employers who expect a net cost increase also are significantly less likely to encourage employees to continue working until they reach their country's statutory retirement age. These effects are in line with our hypothesis that the perceived labour cost-productivity gap affects recruitment and retention behaviour of older workers. The results also show that organisations with a more high-skilled staff are more inclined to retain older workers. This is in line with what one would expect from human capital theory, in the sense that the higher the value of the accumulated knowledge and skills an employee embodies, the more an employer is inclined to retain an older worker. Further, the results show that employers who already have a large proportion of older workers in their staff are more inclined to recruit and retain older workers. Personnel shortages positively influence the recruitment and retention behaviour towards older workers.

5.5.   Conclusions and discussion

Raising the labour force participation of older workers is a key policy objective in the EU. Negative perceptions of employers about older workers' productivity are often assumed to hamper a further increase of their labour force participation (OECD, 2006; Van Dalen et al., 2010a). This study has examined perceptions of European employers regarding the consequences of an ageing personnel structure. Not only the consequences for the organisation's labour productivity, but also perceived consequences for labour costs were examined. The results show that a majority of European employers in each of the countries studied do not expect the ageing of their staff to affect the productivity level within their organisation. With respect to employers' perception of the consequences of ageing on labour costs, the results show much more variation. Many European employers expect labour costs to increase as a result of an ageing staff, but the percentages differ widely across Europe, from 16 per cent in Poland to 75 per cent of Dutch employers. By combining perceptions about labour costs and productivity the survey shows that about half of employers associate ageing personnel with a net cost increase — a situation in which the change in labour costs exceeds the change in productivity. Perceptions of such a gap are not without consequences as they negatively affect both recruitment and retention of older workers.

Table 5.6. Explaining European employers' recruitment and retention of older workers (logistic regression analysis)

| | Behaviour towards older workers | | | |
| | Recruitment | | Retention | |
	Odds ratio	z-value	Odds ratio	z-value
Expected labour cost-productivity gap	0.87**	-2.83	0.91*	-2.36
Control variables				
Sector of industry (industries = reference category):				
Construction	1.04	0.23	1.11	0.78
Services and trade	1.22	1.65	1.07	0.73
Public sector	0.89	-0.83	1.11	0.91
Education, health care and social work	1.22	1.49	1.06	0.55
Organisational features:				
Size (logarithm)	1.23**	7.28	1.15**	5.64
Share of high-skilled workers	1.07	0.40	1.32*	2.13
Share of workers with fixed-term temporary contract	0.75	-1.23	0.83	-0.92
Share of older workers	3.47**	4.89	3.44**	6.00
Extent of absenteeism/ sickness rate	1.06	0.76	0.95	-0.78
Experienced shortages (no shortages = reference category)				
Some vacancies	1.77**	6.09	1.63**	6.43
Many vacancies	2.66**	6.21	1.71**	3.92

Countries (Denmark = reference category):				
France	0.67	-1.73	1.45*	2.22
Germany	0.78	-1.81	0.39**	-7.61
Italy	0.14**	-8.22	0.24**	-9.58
Netherlands	0.62**	-3.40	0.42**	-7.24
Poland	0.87	-0.93	1.29*	2.13
Sweden	0.71*	-1.99	0.65**	-3.17
Pseudo R²	0.08		0.08	
N	4912		4912	

*Significant at $p < .05$; **significant at $p < .01$.
Source: ASPA Employers Survey (2009)

Tenure wages and employment protection are important factors explaining employers' perceptions of a divergence between productivity and labour costs. European employers tend to associate employment protection rules predominantly with a net cost increase, and employers who face a steep tenure wage profile make an association with larger net cost increases than those who face a flat wage profile. Although we find such relationships in each of the countries we studied, the observed differences in perceived employment protection and wage profiles across countries explain the differences in the perceived wage productivity gap between countries only to a limited extent. This raises two interesting issues for further research. First of all, which other country-specific factors influence the perception of a divergence between labour costs and productivity? Future research might focus on age-related fringe benefits, employers' contribution to sickness benefits and other institutional factors. The second issue relates to the variation in perceptions about level of employment protection within countries. Future research might examine the root causes of these different perceptions. For instance, employers may vary in their perception of degree of enforcement of employment protection legislation, or may see more of a problem in laying off workers when the number of union members is high within the organisation.

A final note on the policy implications. The insights generated by this employer study might suggest avenues for policy makers in tackling the problems of ageing labour markets. Our empirical models shed only some light on unravelling the relationship between age, pay and productivity, and many more elements not uncovered seem to play a role. A counterfactual in this study shows that even when employment protection and tenure wage systems are abolished, 40 per cent of employers still expect a net cost increase, compared to the baseline situation where 53 per cent expects such an increase. This suggest that labour market policy must have a wider scope than is usually assumed, and silver-bullet solutions like the abolishment of employment protection are not going to solve all the problems of an ageing labour market. Furthermore, the country-specificity of employer behaviour and perceptions seems to be a hardwired element of most labour market studies, and in that respect it is a silent reminder to policy makers that popular solutions like exporting the Danish model of 'flexicurity' to other countries must be met with some scepticism. Good or best practices are often hard to copy, as the tacit mechanisms of labour markets and organisations will be lost in translation.

6. Employers' policies and practices towards extension of working lives: conclusion, discussion and implications

6.1. Introduction

In most Western countries, macro-level actors realise there are major challenges ahead in dealing with an ageing society. Demographic developments will have large consequences for welfare state expenditures and will profoundly alter the composition and level of labour supply on the labour market. Although various measures to raise the participation levels of older workers have been suggested for a good length of time now, there is still only limited insight into how employers are behaving towards older workers.

This study examined employers' attitudes and behaviour towards older workers. The central questions of this study were (1) whether Dutch employers' behaviour has been changing over time and (2) how European employers are behaving towards older workers, offering the opportunity to analyse behaviour of Dutch employers in a European perspective. To answer these questions, international survey data was jointly collected within the framework of a research project called 'Activating Senior Potential in Ageing Europe' [ASPA]. Consortium partners of the ASPA-project collected survey data among employers in eight European countries: Denmark, France, Germany, Italy, the Netherlands, Poland, Sweden and the United Kingdom. The surveys were sent to company directors, owners and heads of HR departments ('employers'). In the survey 'older workers' were defined as workers aged 50 years and older. Besides survey research, all consortium partners conducted case study research at the organisational level in their own country.

In this chapter, I will summarize the results of the studies in this dissertation (6.2). Furthermore, I will discuss the scientific (6.3) and societal (6.4) relevance of the results. In the final section, I will put forward suggestions for future research (6.5).

6.2. Summary of the results

Between the early 1970s and the mid-1990s, early withdrawal from the labour market increasingly became the *modus operandi* among actors involved. Since the mid-1990s, raising the participation levels of older workers has been one of the key objectives of policy makers in most Western countries (OECD, 2001) and institutional restrictions have limited most early exit behaviour on the supply side. But are *employers* responsive to 'management by speech' from public officials and institutional changes aimed at working longer? This study shows that —although Dutch employers seem to have modestly changed their retention behaviour over the last decade— nowadays still relatively few employers are behaving in a way that actively supports a trend towards working longer. Changes in the institutional restrictions, however, do influence employers' behaviour towards older workers.

In this study, attention is paid to changes in Dutch employers' recruitment and retention behaviour towards older workers over the last decade. In chapter 2, surveys administered to Dutch 'higher managers' in 2000, 2002, 2005, 2008 and 2009 (N=2,833) are being analysed. As shown in this chapter, there is no indication that Dutch employers have become more favourably disposed to recruit older workers over the last decade; recruitment levels of older workers are generally low and seem to change parallel to business-cycle fluctuations. Employers' retention behaviour shows a different picture, as there seems to be a growing tendency among employers to encourage workers to continue working until the official retirement age of 65 years. The results on employers' retention behaviour showed a clear and rather gradual time effect between 2000 and 2008, and even though between 2008 and 2009 (which was the start of the recession) support to retain older workers declined substantially, the retention level was still higher when compared to the period 2000 to 2005.

The results furthermore show that the relative position of older workers compared to other underrepresented groups in the labour market has improved. Whereas the recruitment of female workers, older workers, and non-natives and the reintegration of disabled and partially disabled workers followed the labour market pattern, the only exception to this pattern comes from the increase in employers' efforts in encouraging workers to continue working until age 65, showing a substantial increase over the years 2000 to 2008. Whilst in 2009 all recruitment and retention of personnel plummeted, the relative position of older workers caught up. Nevertheless, older workers are still 'last in line' when it comes to their recruitment.

In the period 2000 to 2009, results show that organisational policies, such as for instance training programs, possibilities of extra leave and ergonomic measures, also followed the business-cycle: a reduction of policies between 2000 and 2005, a revival in 2008, and a reduction in 2009 again. Part-time early retirement was the exception and showed a gradual increase during the period 2000 to 2008 and a small reduction in 2009.

Whereas chapter 2 focused on Dutch employers' recruitment and retention behaviour over time based on survey research —and could therefore address 'how' and 'why' questions only to a limited extent— chapter 3 addresses changes over time by analysing longitudinal case studies conducted in three Dutch organisations. The analyses were based on desk research materials, field notes and a total of 45 interviews with HR officers, managers and employees. This chapter examines views, dilemmas and behaviour from the perspective of both the employer and employees over time. How do business-cycle effects and institutional changes affect for instance training opportunities for older workers, health policies, but also recruitment and retention levels? The results confirm the conclusions from chapter 2 that the business–cycle plays a substantial role in organisational behaviour towards older workers. Economic downturns negatively affect training budgets, recruitment of older workers and retention practices. Dutch employers do not seem to be inclined to look beyond the current economic crisis; their focus is on the current situation and not on the long run.

In addition to the cyclical effects in employers' behaviour towards older workers, chapter 3 shows that changes in the institutional framework have reshaped Dutch employers' behaviour markedly over time. For instance, incited by pressure of safety regulations and the increased costs involved for the employer in case of sick leave or disability leave over the last decade, the study shows an increasing focus on health-related measures in professions with intense physical work. Although maybe not incited by intrinsic motivation to extend working lives, the changes in behaviour contribute to physical sustainability of workers and may improve job opportunities at older ages. Institutional changes regarding early exit arrangements and the debate about raising the official retirement age are of later date, but also in this area the results show some first signs of moderate changes in behaviour. Both employees and employers seem to realise that extension of working lives has become an unavoidable fact. In our study, extension of working lives seems to follow a bottom-up process and seems to be predominantly driven by the financial pressure felt by and the wants and capabilities of the individual worker. Employers seem to be able to find creative short-term solutions when necessary, *e.g.* in redeployment and initiatives to add a few years, although they also feel they have to put up with problems resulting from government policies for which they do not have a solution. So, even though neither employers nor workers endorse public policies to extent working lives and raise retirement ages wholeheartedly, employers and workers do comply.

The studies in chapter 2 and chapter 3 on Dutch employers' behaviour over time seem to indicate that in the Netherlands many employers are not actively supporting extension of working lives. The rather passive stance Dutch employers seem to hold towards working longer is also visible in other European countries. Within the ASPA research project, a questionnaire was developed to provide insight into the attitudes and behaviour of employers. The study in chapter 4 examines employers' recruitment and retention behaviour towards older workers in an international perspective. To that end, I analysed surveys administered to employers in Denmark, France, Germany, Italy, the Netherlands, Poland, Sweden and the United Kingdom in 2009. The total number of completed questionnaires varied per country between N=500 and N=1,087, amounting to a total of N=6,285. Both recruitment and retention levels of older workers are rather low in all of the countries (on average 12 and 27 per cent respectively) and employers' actions to extend working lives have a stronger focus on retention than on recruitment of older workers. Very few employers stimulate working beyond the statutory retirement age by either recruiting or retaining workers beyond this retirement age (13%).

Employers' behaviour towards older workers may stem from various underlying reasons, such as the expected consequences of an ageing staff for the own organisation. The results in chapter 4 and chapter 5 show important outcomes with respect to perceived changes in costs and benefits as the own staff ages. As a positive effect, roughly half of European employers expect an increase in the knowledge base as a consequence of an ageing workforce, and only less than ten per cent expect a decline in the knowledge base. However, from the employers' perspective an increasing knowledge base does not seem to directly translate into higher productivity: a majority of European employers in each of the countries does not expect productivity to be affected by the ageing of their staff, a substantial minority expects a decline of labour productivity and a small minority expects an increase.

With respect to employers' perceptions of the consequences of ageing on labour costs, the results show large variation: in Poland 16 per cent of employers expect labour costs to increase, while in the Netherlands this is 75 per cent. By combining perceptions about labour costs and productivity I show that about half of employers associate ageing personnel with an increasing labour cost-productivity gap (53%). The study in chapter 5 shows that perceptions of such a gap are not without consequences, as they negatively affect employers' recruitment of older workers and their efforts to stimulate older workers to continue working until the official retirement age.

Chapter 4 addresses the question whether expectations regarding the wage-productivity gap are related to organisational policies. Are policies focused on bringing costs and benefits of older workers more in line? Two measures often suggested by scientists and policy makers as a way to bridge the gap between labour costs and productivity are lifelong learning and demotion (Hall and Isabella, 1985; European Commission, 2006). Among employers there seems to be not much enthusiasm for actual implementation of these measures: demotion is applied by 7 per cent of European employers, and additional training for older workers to prevent or counter a decline in productivity is provided by 23 per cent of employers. Furthermore, this chapter addresses the question whether personnel policies undertaken by employers are related to the expected wage-productivity gap. The results show that employers who expect a larger wage-productivity gap do not apply organisational measures to bridge this gap (demotion or training) more often. The results rather show the contrary: employers expecting a larger pay-productivity gap more often apply measures such as early retirement. This outcome suggests that an expected labour cost-productivity gap induces employers to lay-off older workers. As early retirement arrangements can have a positive effect on labour costs, this organisational measure may be rational from the point of view of the employer, but obviously early retirement is not contributing to a trend towards working longer.

Within organisations, employers do not seem to take much action to extend working lives. This raises the question: What do employers expect from public policies? The results in chapter 4 show that employers consider incentives to combine work and retirement to be the most effective governmental measure to increase labour force participation of older workers. The second and third governmental measures employers consider to be most effective are the promotion of lifelong learning and wage subsidies.

In chapter 5 it was shown that about half of European employers associate an ageing workforce with a net labour cost increase (53%). Expected consequences of an ageing staff on the labour cost-productivity gap showed high between-country variation. In the Netherlands, even 74 per cent of employers expect a net labour cost increase as the workforce ages. Based on the idea of contract theories in which wages are lower than productivity at younger ages and older workers' wages exceed their productivity (*cf.* Lazear, 1979), the expected labour cost-productivity gap is expected to be related to employment protection and tenure wages. Employment protection refers to protection of permanent workers against individual dismissal. Tenure wages involve the extent to which, apart from the employee's formal qualifications and his function in the organisation, wages rise with tenure (*i.e.* the number of years that the employee has worked in an organisation).

The results showed that in Europe, 58 per cent of employers report wages to rise with tenure to 'a high' or 'some' extent in their organisation, and these perceived tenure wages are particularly high in the Netherlands and France (78 and 72%, respectively). With respect to employment protection, 56 per cent of employers indicate it is 'difficult' or 'very difficult' to fire a worker with a permanent contract; this perceived level of employment protection is highest in Italy (83%) and the Netherlands (70%). Tenure wages and employment protection were both found to be important factors explaining employers' perceptions of a divergence between productivity and labour costs. European employers tend to associate employment protection rules and a steep tenure wage profile predominantly with a net cost increase. This insight implies the labour cost-productivity gap is partly affected by factors (tenure wages and employment protection) often agreed upon on a level beyond the control of the individual employer, such as in legislation and collective employment agreements.

Nevertheless, although tenure wages and employment protection were indeed found to be important factors explaining the cost-productivity gap, these factors explain the gap only to a limited extent. A counterfactual analysis in this study shows that even when employment protection and tenure wage systems would be abolished, 40 per cent of employers still expect a net cost increase, compared to the baseline situation in which 53 per cent expects such an increase. The insights from this study thus also imply that many more elements still uncovered seem to play a role. A number of other country-specific factors influencing the perceived labour cost-productivity gap may have been omitted in the analysis, such as age-related fringe benefits or employers' contributions to sickness benefits.

6.3.   Scientific relevance

The study's objectives were to advance the existing research literature on 1) whether and how Dutch employers' attitudes and behaviour towards older workers have changed over time and 2) the extent to which employers support the extension of working lives from an internationally comparative perspective.

To start with the first objective, in this study it was acknowledged that changes in employers' attitudes and behaviour towards working longer may be dependent on the macro-level context, such as institutional surroundings and business-cycle effects. The results have shown that business-cycle fluctuations have affected Dutch employers' behaviour towards extension of working lives considerably over time. However, right across this *cyclical* movement the results also revealed a modest *structural* increase of Dutch employers encouraging older workers to continue working until age 65. Complementary to these results obtained from pooled cross-sectional survey data analyses, the conducted case study research among Dutch organisation revealed that these changes seem to be incited to a large extent by institutional restrictions. Especially changes in health and safety related measures, which had been implemented predominantly in the 1990s and early 2000s, have clearly affected Dutch employers' behaviour by now. Changes of early retirement arrangements and the debate on raising the official retirement age are of more recent date, and thus far these changes have less clear-cut effects. The case study research not only underscores the shaping influence of institutions on employers' behaviour, but also the delay between implementation and effect.

Apart from macro-level effects, the study also acknowledged employers' behaviour to depend on *organisational* characteristics. The educational level of the staff, the size of the organisation and share of workers older than 50 years in the organisation play a role in recruitment and retention behaviour towards older workers. For instance, organisations with a higher-skilled staff, larger organisations and organisations with a higher share of older workers tend to encourage their older workers more often to continue working until the statutory retirement age. Also sector differences regarding attitudes, behaviour and policies towards older workers were found to be significant. Although sector differences are present and significant in most analyses, differences between sectors of industries are nevertheless relatively small; this is in line with results from earlier research (Remery *et al.*, 2003; Henkens, 2005). Overall, organisational characteristics were found to be often present and significant, but they do not account for much of the variation in employers' attitudes and behaviour. Apart from macro-level effects and organisational characteristics, future research could consider studying the role of the individual within the organisation in more depth.

From a methodological point of view, it is relevant to note that the case study research has provided insights that could not have been deducted from our survey data, and vice versa. In essence, the two methods revealed different though complementary information on changes in employers' behaviour towards older workers over time. Whereas the survey data showed a significant influence of business-cycle effects on both recruitment and retention behaviour and a structural time effect in retention behaviour, certain underlying developments are not visible in the indicators used. The case study research, on the other hand, does not provide insight into the significance of developments over time, but does provide more information on 'how' and 'why' employers' behaviour over time has been subject to change and provides more insight into more ambivalent developments and underlying motivations of employers' behaviour.

The case study research contributes to research on organisational behaviour towards extension of working lives in several ways. First, it gives insight into changed content of umbrella concepts. Whereas for instance training provisions and health-related measures in organisational survey research may report to *exist* constantly over time, the *extent* and the *content* of practices in this area seem to have evolved substantially. It is very difficult to capture the complexity of such umbrella concepts in survey research. Furthermore, the choices and constraints both managers and employees face regarding extension of working lives are complex and shifting. The use of multiple case studies with both the perspective of managers and employees sheds light on several attitudes and processes resulting from institutional changes in health-related regulations and regulations concerning retirement. Adaptations in health-related regulations seem to have led to marked changed behaviour in organisations in order to meet the new regulations, and the necessary changes are supported by both managers and employees. Regarding changes in early retirement and the retirement age we find more ambiguous attitudes and behavioural changes in the organisations.

Nevertheless, the results from the case study research are to be interpreted analytically and cannot be generalised statistically. The organisations under study were selected as and can still considered to be good practice organisations. Therefore, it may very well be the case that whereas employees and managers in these organisations do find opportunities to extend working lives, individuals in other organisations may have less influence on their timing and manner of retirement.

The study's second objective was to advance the existing research literature on employers supporting extension of working lives from an internationally comparative perspective. This study uses the first large-scale survey among European employers covering all types of European welfare state regimes, offering several opportunities for advancing the research literature. First, on a European level, the extent to which employers support prolongation of working lives and take action to retain older workers is not well documented; a void this study aims to fill. Earlier survey research making cross-national comparisons were mainly descriptive in nature and addressed questions on opinions, attitudes and to a lesser extent practices towards older workers (Guillemard *et al.*, 1996; Van Dalen *et al.*, 2009a; 2010a). In this study, the focus lied with employers' *behaviour* towards older workers and *perceptions* about the consequences of an ageing staff with respect to productivity and labour costs. A second, more general issue is whether perceptions and behaviour towards older workers are tied to a specific national context, or whether perceptions and practices are more widely found among employers in Europe.

In this study, recruitment and retention levels were found to be rather low in general, employers rather retained than recruited older workers and working beyond the statutory age of retirement was not so much encouraged. The results in this study indicate that relatively few employers are behaving in a way that actively supports a trend towards working longer. The international comparison shows that the lack of action from employers to activate senior potential is not a matter of just one specific country, but was widely found among European employers. This does not imply, however, that European employers show a uniform pattern in their attitudes and behaviour towards older workers. In many respects European employers do not seem to follow a 'European way'; national contexts play an important role as well. Even between countries belonging to the same type of welfare state, attitudes and behaviour differ considerably, for instance between Danish and Swedish employers (both belonging to Esping-Andersen's (1990) social-democratic welfare state) and between German and French employers (both belonging to the continental/conservative welfare state type).

This last observation may be relevant for future international-comparative research on employers' behaviour. In scientific cross-national research there is a long and strong tradition of using 'welfare state types' as the main unit of examination. Also in the selection of countries for the ASPA project this welfare state tradition played a major role. Beforehand, it seemed plausible that employers' attitudes and behaviour are more similar between countries belonging to the same type of welfare state. For instance, Social-Democratic welfare states are typically costly and can best be maintained 'with most people working, and the fewest possible living off of social transfers' (Esping-Andersen, 1990, p. 28). One may argue that because these welfare states throughout history have had a mission to mobilise most segments in the population for labour market purposes, employers have also been incited and therefore adopted a different view and more activating behaviour and policies towards older workers than in other European countries. The results in this study seem to indicate that welfare state types do not play a significant role in how *employers* view the consequences of an ageing workforce or behave towards the older workers in their organisation.

In addition, although Scandinavian countries are sometimes considered 'leading countries' for instance in their approach towards lifelong learning and the labour force participation of women and older workers, this study finds no particular 'leading country' when it comes to activating behaviour from the *employers'* side. Although institutions in those countries are apparently effective in increasing labour force participation, employers' attitudes and behaviour towards older workers seem not so different.

Finally, some comments can be made with respect to the theoretical background. Whereas human capital theory assumes that individual earnings are proportional to human capital —in terms of knowledge and skills—, implicit contract theories imply that employers may have implicit contracts with their employees regarding the relationship between productivity and income over the lifetime: earnings are lower than productivity during the first phase of workers' careers and higher than productivity during the second phase.

In this study, it was shown that on the one hand roughly half of employers expect an increase in the knowledge base as a consequence of an ageing staff. On the other hand, a majority of European employers in each of the countries do not expect the ageing of their staff to affect productivity levels, a substantial minority expects a decline of labour productivity and a small minority expects an increase. When combining employers' opinions on the development of productivity and on the knowledge base one may conclude that from the employers' perspective an increasing knowledge base does not seem to translate directly into higher productivity. Or in other words: even though human capital increases, the additional human capital is not necessarily relevant from the perspective of productivity.

From a human capital theory perspective, these results also indicate that in some organisations employers perceive their employees to accumulate capital until a certain threshold and keep this *constant*, employees in some organisations are perceived to generally accumulate human capital over the whole working career, also at older ages (*increase*) and in some organisations human capital is perceived to depreciate at some point in a workers' career (*decline*). Such perceptions may very well depend on for instance the utilization of specific human capital in an organisation or the type of economic activity an organisation is involved in.

6.4.   Societal relevance

In the past decades, reversing the trend towards ever earlier labour force withdrawal is an objective that we find on almost every policy maker's agenda. Whereas in the early 1980s, governments often stimulated the early retirement of older workers, since the mid-1990s governments are trying to reverse this early retirement trend. But even though policymakers at the country level may agree on and be convinced of the necessity to extend working lives, whether this macro-goal can and will actually be achieved depends on individual workers' and employers' behaviour. As shown in this research, most employers have not (yet) adjusted their attitudes and behaviour in a way that reflects a trend towards stimulation of working longer. Recruitment and retention levels of older workers are low in general and organisational policies do not seem to be aimed at facing expected negative consequences of an ageing staff. Furthermore, the case study research suggests that employers do not seem to be inclined to look beyond the current economic crisis — a period of possible labour market shortages. Their focus is on the current situation and not on the long run.

Knowledge of employers' attitudes and actions towards older workers and their views on prolongation of working lives makes it easier to anticipate the feasibility of *governmental* policy measures. The studies over time indicate the significant influence from institutional change on employers' behaviour. The international-comparative studies on employers' views and behaviour provide some leads in what types of measures governments could pursue to increase older workers' labour force participation.

First, the most effective governmental measure to increase labour force participation of older workers —according to European employers— are incentives to combine work and retirement. A preference for such a combination suggests there is room for older workers to work longer, although in an adjusted form. The survey does not address what a 'combination of work and retirement' entails and therefore we do not exactly know what employers have in mind, but one way to combine work and retirement might for instance be in the form of phased retirement. The basic idea of phased (or gradual) retirement is that an older worker gradually reduces work hours and efforts, while remaining with his or her employer. Sometimes partial retirement is distinguished from phased retirement involving a change of employer, although partial retirement is also often used interchangeably with phased retirement (for an overview see for example Kantarci and Van Soest, 2008); the existing literature is not consistent in the use of terminology. Another possibility is bridge employment, which means that older workers work in any form between their career jobs and full retirement, for instance by taking a part-time job or other temporary employment prior to definitive retirement, within the same occupation or in the same position, in a completely different job or in self-employment. Earlier research already indicated that many older workers and retirees are interested in or actually participating in gradual retirement or bridge employment (Cahill *et al.*, 2007; Kantarci and Van Soest, 2008; Henkens *et al.*, 2009; Van Dalen *et al.*, 2009b). Given the national, historical preference for part-time work, solutions along the lines of phased retirement would probably meet considerable public consent in the Netherlands.

Dutch policy makers could examine the effectiveness of policies in other countries, such as in Sweden. In Sweden, people can reduce working hours to a maximum of 50 per cent, while income can be complemented with pension benefits. Some first evaluations indicate that the net effect on labour supply is positive (Wadensjö, 2006). An example of a policy design that was considered less successful comes from Germany. Germany has a Part-time Retirement Law which was enacted in 1996 in order to ease the transition from work to retirement and provide the opportunity to reduce working time for a certain period. An increasing amount of German employees have been using part-time retirement in the past years. At first, this development was considered a success, but later it became clear that many older employees work full-time for the first half of the partial retirement period and then leave for a pre-retirement sabbatical for the other half. So the current design is sometimes considered to be more an instrument for early retirement than a step towards gradual retirement (Frerichs and Aleksandrowicz, 2011).

Secondly, many European employers think the promotion of lifelong learning is an effective governmental measure to increase older workers' labour force participation, although this measure is strikingly less favoured by Dutch employers compared to their European colleagues. Participation in training programs usually decreases with age, and workers older than 50 years hardly participate in such programs (Fouarge and Schils, 2008; Lindley and Duell, 2006; Elias and Davies, 2004; Bassanini et al., 2005; Bishop, 1997). Fouarge and Schils (2008) find that older workers who did participate in formal on-the-job training are less likely to retire early than workers who are not engaged in training activities, which may suggest that investing in training at older ages is indeed a viable measure to keep older workers in paid employment. In the studies in this dissertation I find on the one hand that employers think promotion of lifelong learning is an effective governmental measure to increase older workers' labour force participation, but on the other hand in most countries employers hardly apply training plans for older workers in their own organisation. These results may imply that employers think they cannot or should not be held responsible for the costs of lifelong learning, and believe the government or older workers themselves have to take responsibility for this. Earlier research showed that Dutch employers think employees and employers are mainly responsible for financing lifelong learning (both almost 50%) (Van Dalen et al., 2009b), indicating that Dutch employers do no think the government is responsible for the financial aspects of training.

Thirdly, according to a majority of employers, wage subsidies are effective governmental measures to increase labour force participation of older workers. The larger the labour cost-productivity gap employers expect, the more often employers consider wage subsidies to be an effective measure to increase the labour force participation of older workers. This may suggest that employers expect governments to partly facilitate the process of bridging the gap between pay and productivity. In the Netherlands, some governmental policies in this area were implemented recently. A first measure introduced in 2009 aims at employers and concerns the risk of hiring an older worker that may become ill for a longer period. If an employer hires an older worker (55^+) who has been unemployed or disabled for over a year the employer gets a compensation for the wage costs of this employee if (s)he falls ill for a period over 13 weeks (SZW, 2009). A second measure is an annual reduction of social security contributions in case an employer hires a worker of 50^+ who has been on benefits for a period of three years. An annual reduction is also awarded to employers who continue employing a 62^+ worker. Another measure, also introduced in 2009, should serve as an incentive for employees to keep on working longer. This so-called 'doorwerkbonus' (career continuation bonus) is awarded to older workers in the form of a tax credit if they continue working after the age of 62. This measure has been severely criticized (see *e.g.* Sap *et al.*, 2009), as many economists consider it a deadweight loss: the tax credit goes primarily to people who were to stay in the labour market anyway. Those who suffer from health problems or those who cannot find a job will not and can not qualify for the tax credit. However, many subsidies in the Netherlands are under pressure as the current government —that was elected in September 2012— has plans to abolish these measures or replace them with other measures.

Some other European countries also have experience with employment subsidies, such as Sweden. One particular positively assessed program is called the Plus Job Scheme, which provides recruitment subsidies aimed at enhancing the employability and labour market prospect of vulnerable groups, including older workers. Evaluations of these recruitment subsidies provide reason to believe that these wage subsidies have been successful in terms of unemployed (re-)-entering the labour market and improving employability, while negative side effects such as deadweight loss, crowding out, creaming and displacement effect appear to have been limited (Anxo and Ericson, 2011; Anxo, 2008).

Besides governments, *organisations* may also benefit from knowledge of employers' policies and practices towards older workers when developing and introducing personnel policies. In this study we find that many employers expect an increasing labour cost-productivity gap due to ageing of their staff, which is negatively related to recruitment and retention behaviour. Nevertheless, not many organisations have implemented personnel policies that seem to be aimed at tackling the wage-productivity gap.

One suggestion that is often put forward by scientists and policy makers as a way to bridge the gap between labour costs and productivity is to demote older workers. In other words, older workers step back in terms of position and salary at the end of their careers. Demotion touches upon both elements of an increasing labour cost-productivity gap. If organisations and employees have a culture in which demotion is open for discussion and is not perceived as a kind of 'failure', demotion offers a way to bring back balance between labour costs and productivity at later stages of someone's career and therefore a useful instrument for increasing older workers' labour force participation. In practice, this might point towards solutions along the lines of bridge employment. Research from Henkens *et al.* (2012) shows that bridge employment is becoming more and more common and shows a large variety in shapes and forms. An important characteristic of bridge employment is the flexibility of contracts and also remuneration shows a downward flexibility that is 'unusual' with respect to older workers. A majority of older workers in bridge employment have an hourly wage that was lower than in their previous job. For employers bridge employment might offer opportunities to rebalance productivity and remuneration.

Although in some professions a decline in productivity may play a role, it is not at all certain whether the productivity of older workers declines after a certain age; research outcomes in the area are still inconclusive (see for an overview for example Skirbekk, 2008). In case a productivity decline at older ages is not necessarily to be expected and demotion is considered to lead to unmotivated workers, measures which result in a flatter age-income profile are probably a good alternative to demotion to increase the financial sustainability of an ageing organisation. In most organisations, wage systems are negotiated on a level beyond the individual employers' control and are dealt with at the meso-level. Some European countries already have experience with flattening the age-income profile. For instance in Denmark, off the late 1990s the bargaining system has been decentralised and the number of steps on the wage ladder was reduced markedly. In Denmark wages have increasingly been determined by qualifications, productivity, function and responsibility, while the importance of seniority has decreased (Jensen and Madsen, 2011).

Also for employers' associations the results of this research are of relevance. Although employers' associations generally support raising the official retirement age in the Netherlands, many (individual) employers have not yet implemented corresponding personnel policies in their own organisation. Employers' associations may want to play a role in giving practical effect to personnel policies aimed at facing the consequences of an ageing workforce and disseminate for instance suitable possibilities on combinations of work and retirement in organisations.

Finally, the study provides more insight into *older people's* possibilities to (re-) enter or stay on the labour market. The case study research shows that employees have a risk of getting 'stuck' between on the one hand institutional changes that restrict early retirement, while on the other hand they have to deal with employers who are not typically inclined to attract and retain older workers for their organisations. Employers' current behaviour towards older workers may make it worthwhile for older workers to consider taking matters in their own hands and think about their own employability in good time. If working longer is the new reality, what can older workers do themselves to stay employable? Taking care of the own physical and cognitive productivity is one option, but other options may include to orient towards and discuss preventive transitions, phased retirement or bridge employment opportunities in time. Second, many issues may ideally be discussed at the organisational level between employers and united employees, rather than at the individual level. Works councils may want to commit themselves to give practical effect to sustainability of careers by actively bringing together employers and employees to think about for instance suitable possibilities of combining work and retirement in the organisation.

6.5. Discussion

In this final section, I discuss methodological strengths as well as limitations of this study and put forward suggestions for future research. To start with one of the strengths: the study addresses the *employers'* perspective on the extension of working lives, a perspective that is often neglected in the scientific literature. But also in terms of societal relevance it is of vital importance to address issues on the demand side, as employers are one of the key players in defining opportunities for extension of working lives. Another strength of the study is that it uses internationally comparable survey data from over 6,000 employers in countries from all parts of Europe. This data offers a unique opportunity to study employers' attitudes and behaviour towards older workers in-depth, including the possibility to analyse cross-national differences as well as differences between all sectors of industries and organisational sizes. Finally, the combination of both survey research and case study research provides insight in both questions on incidence and trends of employers' behaviour as well as more ambivalent developments and underlying motivations.

An important limitation is that the survey research suffers —as do many other corporate surveys— from low response rates, which may give rise to biased results. In case one assumes a higher response among organisations holding negative stereotypes concerning older workers or having less confidence in a future with an ageing workforce, the results might be biased by employers 'ventilating' their discontent. In this case, results on behaviour are likely to underestimate recruitment and retention of older workers and positive perceptions, and overestimate negative perceptions. In case a higher response among 'good practice' organisations is assumed, results on behaviour are likely to overestimate recruitment, retention and organisational policies applied, while underestimating negative perceptions. Although this study already paid extensive attention to procedural equivalence, some possible source of bias —especially at the data collection phase— are virtually unavoidable. Future studies may want to continue giving specific attention to equivalence in the process of international data collection to obtain the highest possible equivalence, but may also want to engage in for instance non-response analyses.

Another limitation is that this study is based on employers' perceptions regarding an ageing staff and self-reported behaviour towards older workers. The study has shown that the dominant consequence of the ageing of the workforce is perceived to be a growing gap between labour costs and productivity. A logical next question is whether these perceived consequences are accurate, or whether employers underestimate or overestimate the development of labour costs and productivity as the workforce ages. Future researchers may therefore want to combine employers' perceptions about developments in labour costs and productivity and actual measures within organisations. With respect to self-reported behaviour, the study has shown that European employers are little involved in extending older workers' careers. Self-reported behaviour is more likely to be an overestimation (due to expected desirability of specific answers) than an underestimation, but to assess the accuracy of employers' reporting, future studies may want to combine self-reported behaviour with direct measures of hiring and retention behaviour.

There are a number of issues that have received no or only limited attention in this study, but deserve to be considered in future research. First, this study examined whether employers' behaviour has been changing *over time*. Analyses on changes in attitudes and behaviour over time would benefit from a panel design, in which the same cross-section of employers is surveyed and repeated observations of the same variables are collected over a period of time. Following the same employers over time provides more opportunities to study causality, which helps to achieve a thorough understanding of what is driving employers' behaviour.

Second, this study examined *European* employers' views and behaviour towards older workers. Although the number of countries (eight) is informative for this —more exploratory— study, future studies might want to consider involving more or less countries; depending on the question the researcher wants to address. The number of countries in this study is too small to perform multilevel analyses to test for macro-level effects, so in case future researchers want to examine organisational behaviour and institutional effects within a multilevel framework, the number of countries should be extended considerably. But future research might also want to embark on in-depth country comparisons with specific countries.

The ageing of the population and the financial crisis evolving at the same time poses an unprecedented dilemma upon employers: while retention of older workers is probably desirable in the long run, in the short run employers have to survive one of the largest recessions since the thirties of the previous century. When older workers (have to) leave the labour market this is often definite and for many older workers dismissal means they will be long-term unemployed (Corpeleijn, 2009; Van Dalen *et al.*, 2009b). Dismissal or early retirement of older workers may involve a 'relief' for organisations in the short run, but a virtually permanent loss of knowledge and skills of older workers in the long run. Besides these developments, institutions increasingly have been forming restrictions to leave the workforce early.

While the current debate about raising the statutory retirement age is understandable from the perspective of the financial sustainability of the Dutch welfare state, the discussion obscures the view on underlying problems regarding older workers. An increase in the number of older —and relatively highly paid— workers reduces the financial sustainability of an organisation and therefore increases incentives for organisations to either decrease older workers' wages, to renegotiate tasks and terms, or to let older workers go. As long as concepts like demotion, competence-based remuneration, bridge employment and phased retirement are non-negotiable or meet barriers, the answer to how employers can profitably employ older workers remains complex.

References

Addison, J.T. and P. Teixeira (2003), The economics of employment protection. *Journal of Labor Research*, 24(1), 85-129.

Antikainen, A. (2001), Is lifelong learning becoming a reality? The case of Finland from a comparative perspective. *European Journal of Education*, 36(3), 379-94.

Anxo, D. (2008), Innovative labour market policies and practices: Plus job scheme for long-term unemployed people. *European Employment Observatory*, Spring 2008. Brussels: European Commission.

Anxo, D. and T. Ericson (2011), *Senior workers participation in the labour market and public policies: The Swedish case*. ASPA country report, deliverable 2.2.

Arts, W.A. and J.P.T.M. Gelissen (2002), Three worlds of welfare capitalism or more? A state-of-the-art report. *Journal of European Social Policy*, 12(2), 137-158.

ASPA, Employers Survey, (2009), The Hague: Netherlands Interdisciplinary Demographic Institute.

Aubert, P. and B. Crépon (2007), Are older workers less productive? Firm-level evidence on age-productivity and age-wage profiles. Paris: Mimeo, INSEE.

Baltes, P.B., U.M. Staudinger and U. Lindenberger (1999), Lifespan psychology: Theory and application to intellectual functioning. *Annual Review of Psychology*, 50, 471-507.

Barth, M.C., W. McNaught and P. Rizzi (1993), Corporations and the ageing workforce. In P.H. Mirvis (ed.), *Building the competitive workforce: Investing in human capital for corporate success*. New York, NY: Wiley and Sons, 156-200.

Bassanini, A., A. Booth, G. Brunello, M. De Paola and E. Leuven (2005), Workplace training in Europe. Bonn: IZA Discussion Paper, No. 1640.

Becker, G.S. (1962), Investment in human capital: A theoretical analysis. *Journal of Political Economy*, 70(5), 9-49.

Belot, M., J. Boone and J.C. van Ours (2002), Welfare effects of employment protection. Discussion Paper No. 3396. London: CEPR

Berger, E.D. (2009), Managing age discrimination: an examination of the techniques used when seeking employment. *The Gerontologist*, 49(3), 317-32.

Bishop, J. (1997), What we know about employer-provided training: A review of the literature. *Research in Labor Economics*, 16, 19-87.

Blanchard, O.J. (2004). The economic future of Europe. *Journal of Economic Perspectives*, 18(4), 3-26.

Blundell, R., C. Meghir and S. Smith (2002), Pension incentives and the pattern of early retirement. *Economic Journal*, 112(478), C153-C170.

Boeri, T. and J.F. Jimeno (2005), The effects of employment protection: Learning from variable enforcement. *European Economic Review*, 49(8), 2057-77.

Bonoli, G. (1997), Classifying welfare states: A two-dimension approach. *Journal of Social Policy*, 26(3), 351-72.

Bound, J., M. Schoenbaum, T. Stinebrickner and T. Waidmann (1999), The dynamic effects of health on the labor force transitions of older workers. *Labour Economics*, 6(2), 179-202.

Brewster, C., A. Hegewisch, L. Mayne and O. Tregaskis (1994), Methodology of the Price Waterhouse Cranfield project. In: C. Brewster and A. Hegewisch (eds), *Policy and practice in European human resource management*. London: Routledge, 230-45.

Brooke, L. (2009), Prolonging the careers of older information technology workers: Continuity, exit or retirement transitions? *Ageing & Society*, 29(2), 237-56.

Brooke, L. and P. Taylor (2005), Older workers and employment: Managing age relations. *Ageing & Society*, 25(3), 415-29.

Cahill, K.E., M.D. Giandrea and J.F. Quinn (2006), Retirement patterns from career Employment. *The Gerontologist*, 46(4), 514-23.

Cahill, K.E., M.D. Giandrea and J.F. Quinn (2007), Down shifting: The role of bridge jobs after career employment. April 2007, Issue Brief 6. Boston College: Center on Aging & Work.

Casey, B. and R. Lindly (2011), *Older worker labour force participation and policy in the UK*. ASPA country report, deliverable 2.2.

Checcucci, P., M. Di Rosa, G. Lamura and A. Principi (2011), *Senior workers participation in the labour market and public policies: The Italian case*. ASPA country report, deliverable 2.2.

Chiu, W.C.K., A.W. Chan, E. Snape and T. Redman (2001), Age stereotypes and discriminatory attitudes towards older workers: An East-West comparison. *Human Relations*, 54(5), 629-61.

Conen, W.S., K. Henkens and J.J. Schippers (2011), Are employers changing their behavior toward older workers? An analysis of employers' surveys 2000-2009. *Journal of Aging & Social Policy*, 23(2), 141-58.

Conen, W.S., K. Henkens and J.J. Schippers (2012), Employers' attitudes and actions towards the extension of working lives in Europe. *International Journal of Manpower*, 33(6), 648-665.

Corpeleijn, A. (2009), Werkhervatting na ontslag: een vergelijking van oudere en jongere werknemers, *Sociaaleconomische trends*, 2e kwartaal, 35-40.

CPB (2000), *Ageing in the Netherlands*. The Hague: CPB.

Crépon, B., N. Deniau and S. Pérez-Duarte (2002), Wages, productivity and worker characteristics: A French perspective. Paris: Mimeo, INSEE.

Dalen, H.P. van, K. Henkens and J. Schippers (2009a), Dealing with older workers in Europe: A comparative survey of employers' attitudes and actions. *Journal of European Social Policy*, 19(1), 47-60.

Dalen, H.P. van, C.J.I.M. Henkens, B. Lokhorst and J. Schippers (2009b), *Herintreding van vroeggepensioneerden*. Onderzoek uitgevoerd door het OSA Institute for Labour Studies, Nederlands Interdisciplinair Demografisch Instituut en Expertisecentrum LEEFtijd in opdracht van de Raad voor Werk en Inkomen. Den Haag: Raad voor Werk en Inkomen (RWI), 61p.

Dalen, H.P. van, K. Henkens and J. Schippers (2010a), Productivity of older workers: perceptions of employers and employees. *Population and Development Review,* 36(2), 309-30.

Dalen, H. van, K. Henkens and J. Schippers (2010b), How do employers cope with an ageing workforce? Views from employers and employees. *Demographic Research,* 22(32), 1015-36.

Damman, M., K. Henkens and M. Kalmijn (2011), The impact of midlife educational, work, health and family experiences on men's early retirement. *Journal of Gerontology: psychological sciences,* 66(5), 617-627.

Deelen, A. (2011), Wage-tenure profiles and mobility. Discussion Paper No. 198. The Hague: CPB.

DiMaggio, P.J. and W.W. Powell (1983), The iron cage revisited: Institutional isomorphism and collective rationality in organizational fields. *American Sociological Review,* 48(2), 147-160.

Dorn, D. and A. Sousa-Poza (2005), Early retirement: Free choice or forced decision? *CESifo Working Paper No.* 1542. Germany, Munich: CESifo.

Drury, E. (2001), Ageing in employment: A proposal for a European code of good practice. *The Geneva Papers on Risk and Insurance,* 26(4), 611-622.

Edgar, F. and A. Geare (2009), Inside the 'black box' and 'HRM'. *International Journal of Manpower,* 30(3), 220-36.

Elias, P. and R. Davies (2004), Employer provided training within the European Union: A comparative review. In: C. Sofer (ed.) *Human capital over the life cycle: A European perspective.* Cheltenham: Edward Elgar.

Employment Taskforce (2003), *Jobs, jobs, jobs. Creating more employment in Europe.* Report of the Employment Taskforce chaired by Wim Kok. Brussels.

Eschtruth, A.D., S.A. Sass and J. Aubry (2007), Employers lukewarm about retaining older workers. Work opportunities for older Americans series 10. Chestnut Hill, MA: Center for Retirement Research at Boston College.

Equal Treatment Commission (2007), *Annual report 2007.* Utrecht: Equal Treatment Commission.

Esping-Andersen, G. (1990), *The three worlds of welfare capitalism.* Oxford: Polity Press.

European Central Bank (2008), *Labour supply and employment in the Euro area countries. Developments and challenges.* Occasional paper series, No. 87/ June 2008.

European Commission (2002), *Report requested by Stockholm European council: 'Increasing labour force participation and promoting active ageing'.* Brussels: European Commission.

European Commission (2004), *Increasing the employment of older workers and delaying the exit from the labor market.* COM 146 final. Brussels: European Commission.

European Commission (2005), *Confronting demographic change: A new solidarity between the generations.* Green paper. COM 94 final. Brussels: European Commission.

European Commission (2006), *The demographic future of Europe – from challenge to opportunity.* Brussels: European Commission.

European Commission (2008a), *Renewed social agenda: Opportunities, access and solidarity in 21st century Europe.* COM 412 final. Brussels: European Commission.

European Commission (2008b), *Demography report 2008: Meeting social needs in an ageing society.* SEC 2911. Brussels: European Commission.

European Commission (2011a), *The 2012 ageing report: Underlying assumptions and projection methodologies.* Brussels: European Commission.

European Commission (2011b), *Employment and social developments in Europe 2011.* Brussels: European Commission.

European Commission (2012). Retrieved September 24, 2012 from the *European year for active ageing and solidarity between generations.* Website: http://europa.eu/ ey2012/.

European Council (2001), *Presidency conclusions.* Stockholm 23 and 24 March. Brussels.

European Council (2002), *Presidency conclusions.* Barcelona 15 and 16 March. Brussels.

European foundation for the improvement of living and working conditions (1999), *Active strategies for an ageing workforce.* Conference Report Turku, 12-13 August. Dublin: European foundation for the improvement of living and working conditions.

European foundation. for the improvement of living and working conditions (2006). Database, available at: http://www.eurofound.europa.eu/areas/ populationandsociety/ageingworkforce.htm (accessed: 9 March 2012).

Eurostat (1990), *Statistical classification of economic activities in the European Community.* NACE Rev. 1. Luxembourg: Eurostat.

Eurostat (2002), *Statistical classification of economic activities in the European Community*, Rev. 1.1. Luxembourg: Eurostat Metadata.

Eurostat (2010), *Labour force survey.* Luxembourg: Eurostat Database.

Eurostat (2012), *Labour force survey.* Luxembourg: Eurostat Database.

Euwals, R., R. de Mooij and D. van Vuuren (2009), *Rethinking retirement.* The Hague: CPB Report.

Ferrera, M. (1996), The 'Southern' model of welfare in social Europe. *Journal of European Social Policy*, 6(1), 17-37.

Flabbi, L. and A. Ichino (2001), Productivity, seniority and wages: new evidence from personnel data. *Labour Economics*, 8(3), 359-87.

Forte, C.S. and C.L. Hansvick (1999), Applicant age as a subjective employability factor: A study of workers over and under age fifty. *Journal of Employment Counseling*, 36,(1), 24-34.

Fouarge, D. and T. Schils (2008), *Training older workers: Does it help make them work longer?* Tilburg: OSA-Publication, A230.

Frerichs, F. and R. Lindley (2009), *Case studies in labour organisations. Orientation and literature review.* ASPA report, deliverable 4.1.

Frerichs, F. and P. Alexandrowicz (2011), *Senior workers participation in the labour market and public policies: The German case.* ASPA country report, deliverable 2.2.

Frerichs, F., R. Lindley, P. Alexandrowicz, B. Baldauf and S. Galloway (2012), Active ageing in organisations: A case study approach. *International Journal of Manpower,* 33(6), 666-684.

Government of the Netherlands (2012), *Stabiliteitsprogramma Nederland.* The Hague: Rijksoverheid.

Gray, L. and J. McGregor (2003), Human resource development and older workers: Stereotypes in New Zealand. *Asia Pacific Journal of Human Resources,* 41(3), 338-53.

Grey Works (2006), *Zestien winnaars laten de jaren tellen. Senior Power Prijs 2006.* The Hague: Grey Works.

Grey Works (2007), *Meer winnaars. Senior power prijs 2007.* The Hague: Grey Works.

Grossman, H. (1977), Risk shifting and reliability in labor markets. *Scandinavian Journal of Economics,* 79(2), 187-209.

Gruber, J. and D. Wise (2002), Social security programs and retirement around the world: Micro estimation. *NBER Working Paper 9407.* Cambridge: NBER.

Guillemard, A., P. Taylor and A. Walker (1996), Managing an ageing workforce in Britain and France. *Geneva papers on risk and insurance – issues and practice,* 21 (4), 478-501.

Guillemard, A. and A. Jolivet (2011), *France: Struggling to find a way out of the early exit culture.* ASPA country report, deliverable 2.2.

Hall, D.T. and L.A. Isabella (1985), Downward movement and career development. *Organizational Dynamics,* 14 (1), 5-23.

Harris, M. and B. Holmstrom (1982), A theory of wage dynamics. *Review of Economic Studies,* 49(3), 315-33.

Hayward, M.D., S. Friedman and H. Chen (1998), Career trajectories and older men's retirement. *The Journals of Gerontology. Series B: Psychological Sciences and Social Sciences,* 53(2), 91-103.

Hayward, M.D., M.A. Hardy and M.C. Liu (1994), Work after retirement: The experiences of older men in the United States. *Social Science Research,* 23(1), 82-107.

Hellerstein, J.K. and D. Neumark (2004), Production function and wage equation estimation with heterogeneous labor: Evidence from a new matched employer-employee data set. Working Paper Series No. 13. Cambridge, MA: NBER, 345-71.

Henkens, K. (1998), *Older workers in transition.* Studies on the early retirement decision in the Netherlands. Dissertation: Universiteit Utrecht.

Henkens, K. (2005), Stereotyping older workers and retirement: The managers' point of view. *Canadian Journal on Aging*, 24(4), 353-66.

Henkens, K., C. Remery and J. Schippers (2008), Shortages in the labour market: An analysis of employers' behaviour. *International Journal of Human Resource Management*, 19(7), 1314-1327.

Henkens, K., H.P. van Dalen and H. van Solinge (2009), *De vervagende grens tussen werk en pensioen: over doorwerkers, doorstarters en herintreders*. Amsterdam: KNAW Press.

Henkens, K., H. van Solinge and H.P. van Dalen (2012), *Doorwerken over de drempel van pensioen*. Amsterdam: KNAW Press.

Hidding, R., A. de Jong, M. Krestin, T. Severijnen, H. Tromp, M. Vermeulen, L. Visman and J. Zuijdervliet (2004), *De oudere werknemer. Omgaan met vergrijzing in de organisatie*. Hoofddorp: STECR.

Horn, J.L. and R.B. Catell (1967), Age differences in fluid and crystallized intelligence. *Acta Psychologica*, 26(2), 107-29.

Hutchens, R.M. (1989), Seniority, wages and productivity: A turbulent decade. *Journal of Economic Perspectives*, 3(4), 49-64.

Ilmakunnas, P., M. Maliranta and J. Vainiomäki (2004), The role of employer and employee characteristics for plant productivity. *Journal of Productivity Analysis*, 21(3), 249-76.

Ilmakunnas, P. and M. Maliranta (2005), Technology, worker characteristics, and wage-productivity gaps. *Oxford Bulletin of Economics and Statistics*, 67(5), 623-45.

Imhoff, E. van and K. Henkens (1998), The budgetary dilemmas of an aging workforce: A scenario analysis for the public sector in the Netherlands. *European Journal of Population*, 14(1), 39-59.

Isaksson, K. and G. Johansson (2000), Adaptation to continued work and early retirement following downsizing: Long-term effects and gender differences. *Journal of Occupational and Organizational Psychology*, 73(2), 241-56.

Jensen, P.H. and P.T. Madsen (2011), *From passive to active approaches in Danish senior policies*. ASPA country report, deliverable 2.2.

Jepsen, M., D. Foden and M. Hutsebaut (eds.) (2002), *Active strategies for older workers*. European Trade Union Institute. Brussels: ETUI.

Jepsen, M., D. Foden and M. Hutsebaut (eds.) (2003), *A lifelong strategy for active ageing*. European Trade Union Institute. Brussels: ETUI.

Johnson, R.W., J. Kawachi and E.K. Lewis (2009), *Older workers on the move: Recareering in later life*. Washington, DC.: AARP, Public Policy Institute.

Jones, B. (2005), Age and great invention. Working Paper Series No. 11359. Cambridge, MA.: National Bureau of Economic Research.

Kalleberg, A.L., D. Knoke, P. Marsden and J. Spaeth (1996), *Organizations in America: Analyzing their structures and human resource practices*. London: Sage Publications.

Kalwij, A. and F. Vermeulen (2008), Health and labour force participation of older people in Europe: What do objective health indicators add to the analysis? *Health Economics*, 17(5), 619-638.

Kantarci, T. and A.H.O. van Soest (2008), Gradual retirement: Preferences and limitations. *De Economist*, 156(2), 113-144.

Karpinska, K., K. Henkens and J. Schippers (2011), The recruitment of early retirees: A vignette study of the factors that affect managers' decisions. *Ageing & Society*, 31(4), 570-589.

Keeter, S., C. Kennedy, M. Dimock, J. Best and P. Craighill (2006), Gauging the impact of growing nonresponse on estimates from a national RDD telephone survey. *Public Opinion Quarterly*, 70(5), 759-79.

Khiji, S.E. and X. Wang (2006), 'Intended' and 'Implemented' HRM: The missing linchpin in strategic human resource management. *The International Journal of Human Resource Management*, 17(7), 1171-89.

Klosse, S. and J. Schippers (2008), The integration of older workers in European labour markets: between macro desires and micro reality. In: F. Pennings, Y. Konijn and A. Veldman (eds.). *Social responsibility in labour relations*. Alphen aan den Rijn: Kluwer Law International, 391-411.

Koppes, L.L.J., E.M.M. de Vroome, M.E.M. Mol, B.J.M. Janssen and S.N.J. van den Bossche (2009), *Nationale enquête arbeidsomstandigheden 2008* ('National survey labor conditions, 2008'). Delft: TNO.

Kotlikoff, L.J. and J. Gokhale (1992), Estimating a firm's age-productivity profile using the present value of workers' earning. *Quarterly Journal of Economics*, 107(4), 1215-42.

Lazear, E.P. (1979), Why is there mandatory retirement? *Journal of Political Economy*, 87(6), 1261-74.

Lehman, H.C. (1953), *Age and achievement*. Princeton, NJ.: Princeton University Press.

Leibfried, S. (1992), Towards a European welfare state? On integrating poverty regimes into the European community. In: Z. Ferge and J.E. Kolberg (eds), *Social policy in a changing Europe*. Frankfurt am Main: Campus Verlag, 245-79.

Lindley, R. and N. Duell (eds.) (2006), *Ageing and employment – identification of good practice to increase job opportunities and maintain older workers in employment*. Final Report, Warwick Institute for Employment Research. Munich: University of Warwick and Economix Research & Consulting.

Loretto, W., C. Duncan and P.J. White (2000), Ageism and employment: controversies, ambiguities and younger people's perceptions. *Aging and Society*, 20(3), 279-302.

Lyon, P. and D. Pollard (1997), Perceptions of the older employee: Is anything really changing? *Personnel Review*, 26(4), 245-257.

Maas, C.J.M. and J.J. Hox (2005), Sufficient sample sizes for multilevel modelling. *Methodology: European Journal of Research Methods for the Behavioral and Social Sciences*, 1(3), 85-91.

Mandl, I., A. Dor and T. Oberholzner (2006), *Age and employment in the new Member States*. Dublin: European Foundation for the Improvement of Living and Working Conditions.

McGregor, J. and L. Gray (2002), Stereotypes and older workers: The New Zealand experience. *Social Policy Journal of New Zealand*, 18, 163-177.

Ministry of Social Affairs and Employment (2012), http://www.rijksoverheid.nl/ministeries/szw (Accessed: 7 June 2012).

Molinié, A. (2003), *Age and working conditions in the European Union*. Dublin: European Foundation for the Improvement of Living and Working Conditions.

Naegele, G and A. Walker (2006), *A guide to good practice in age management*. Luxembourg: European Foundation for the Improvement of Living and Working Conditions.

Nauta, A., M.R. de Bruin and R. Cremer (2004), *De mythe doorbroken. Gezondheid en inzetbaarheid oudere werknemers*. Hoofddorp: TNO Arbeid.

Nimwegen, N. van and R. van der Erf (eds.) (2010), *Demography Monitor 2008; demographic trends, socio-economic impacts and policy implications in the European Union*. NIDI report nr. 82. Amsterdam: KNAW Press.

OECD (ed.) (1998), Work-force ageing in OECD countries. *Employment outlook 1998*. Paris: OECD Publishing, 123-51.

OECD (2000), *Reforms in an ageing society*. Paris.

OECD (2001), *Ageing and income – financial resources and retirement in 9 OECD Countries*, Paris: OECD.

OECD (ed.) (2004), Employment protection regulation and labour market performance. *Employment Outlook 2004*, Paris: OECD Publishing, 61-125.

OECD (ed.) (2006), *Live longer, work longer*. Paris: OECD Publishing.

OECD (2010a), *Education at a glance 2010*. Paris: OECD Publishing.

OECD (2010b), OECD *Indicators on employment protection*. Paris: OECD Publishing.

OECD (2011), Statistics on average effective age of retirement (time series). Retrieved September 24, 2012, from the website: http://www.oecd.org/insurance/pensionsystems/ageingandemploymentpolicies-statisticsonaverageeffectiveageofretirement.htm

Ours, J.C. van and L. Stoeldraijer (2011), Age, wage and productivity in Dutch manufacturing. *De Economist*, 159(2), 113-37.

Perek-Bialas, J. and K. Turek (2011), *Senior workers participation in the labour market and public policies: The Polish case*. ASPA country report, deliverable 2.2.

Phelps, E.S. (1970), *Microeconomic foundations of employment and inflation theory*. London: Macmillan.

Phelps, E.S. (1972), The statistical theory of racism and sexism. *American Economic Review*, 62(4), 659-61.

Pierre, P. and S. Scarpetta (2006), Employment protection: Do firms' perceptions match with legislation? *Economics Letters*, 90(3), 328-34.

Polachek, S.W. and W.S. Siebert (1993), *The Economics of earnings*. Cambridge: Cambridge University Press.

Raymo, J.M., J.R. Warren, M.M. Sweeney, R.M. Hauser and J.-H. Ho (2010), Later-life employment preferences and outcomes: The role of midlife work experiences. *Research on Aging*, 32(4), 419-466.

Raymo, J.M., J.R. Warren, M.M. Sweeney, R.M. Hauser and J.-H. Ho (2011), Precarious employment, bad jobs, labor unions, and early retirement. *The Journals of Gerontology*. Series B: Psychological Sciences and Social Sciences, 66(2), 249-259.

Remery, C., K. Henkens, J.J. Schippers and P. Ekamper (2003), Managing an ageing workforce and a tight labor market: Views held by Dutch employers. *Population Research and Policy Review*, 22(1), 21-40.

Sap, J., J. Schippers and J. Nijssen (2009), *Langer doorwerken en flexibel pensioen*. Netspar NEA Papers, no 23. Tilburg: Netspar.

Siebert, H. (1997), Labor market rigidities: at the root of unemployment in Europe. *Journal of Economic Perspectives*, 11(3), 37-54.

Skirbekk, V. (2008), Age and productivity potential: A new approach based on ability levels and industry-wide task demand. *Population and Development Review*, 34, Supplement, 191-207.

Solinge, H. van and K. Henkens (2007), Involuntary retirement: The role of restrictive circumstances, timing, and social embeddedness. *The Journals of Gerontology, series B: Psychological Sciences and Social Sciences*, 62(5) S295-S303.

Steinberg, M., K. Donald, J. Najman and H. Skerman (1996), Attitudes of employees and employers towards older workers in a climate of anti-discrimination. *Australasian Journal on Ageing*, 15(4), 154-158.

SZW, Ministry of Social Affairs and Employment (1991), *Ouderenbeleid in arbeidsorganisaties*. The Hague: Ministry of SZW/Loontechnische Dienst.

SZW (2009), *Ongekende mogelijkheden*. Overzicht van de mogelijkheden bij het in dienst nemen van 45-plussers. Den Haag: Ministerie van Sociale Zaken en Werkgelegenheid.

Taylor, P. (2006), *Employment initiatives for an ageing workforce in the EU 15*. Luxembourg: Office for Official Publications of the European Communities.

Taylor, P., L. Brooke, C. McLoughlin and T. Di Biase (2010), Older workers and organizational change: Corporate memory versus potentiality. *International Journal of Manpower*, 31(3), 374-86.

Taylor, P. and A. Walker (1994), The ageing workforce: Employers' attitudes towards older people. *Work, Employment and Society*, 8(4), 569-591.

Taylor, P. and A. Walker (1998), Employers and older workers: Attitudes and employment practices. *Ageing and Society*, 18(6), 641-58.

Thurow, L.C. (1975), *Generating inequality: Mechanisms of distribution in the U.S.* New York, NY: Basic Books.

United Nations (2007), *World economic and social survey 2007*. Development in an ageing world. New York: United Nations Publication.

Vickerstaff, S., J. Cox and L. Keen (2003), Employers and the management of retirement. *Social Policy & Administration*, 37(3), 271-87.

Vickerstaff, S. (2006a), Entering the retirement zone: How much choice do individuals have?' *Social Policy & Society*, 5(4), 507-17.

Vickerstaff, S. (2006b), 'I'd rather keep running to the end and then jump off the cliff'. Retirement decisions: Who decides? *Journal of Social Policy*, 35(3), 455-72.

Wadensjö, E. (2006), *Part-time pensions and part-time work in Sweden*. IZA discussion paper no. 2273. Bonn: Institute for the Study of Labor.

Walker, A. and P. Taylor (1998), *Combating age barriers in employment: A European portfolio of good practice*. Luxembourg: Office for Official Publications of the European Communities.

Walker, A. (1997), *Combating age barriers in job-recruitment and training: European Research Report*. Luxembourg: Office for official Publications of the European Commission.

Walker, A. (1999), *Managing an ageing workforce. A guide to good practice*. Luxembourg: Office for official Publications of the European Commission.

Wang, M., Y. Zhan, S. Liu and K.S. Shultz (2008), Antecedents of bridge employment: A longitudinal investigation. *Journal of Applied Psychology*, 93(4), 818-830.

Wang, M. and K.S. Shultz (2010), Employee retirement: A review and recommendations for future investigation. *Journal of Management*, 36(1), 172-206.

Yin, R.K. (2009), *Case study research: design and methods*. Los Angeles: Sage.

Appendix

Table A.1. Descriptive characteristics of samples used

Country	N	Response rate %	Method
Denmark	609	28	CAWI
France	500	7	CATI
Germany	892	11	PAPI
Italy	770	17	CATI
Netherlands	1,077	23	PAPI
Poland	1,037	23	CATI
Sweden	525	53	PAPI
UK	412	22	CATI

Table A.2. Explaining expected labour cost-productivity gap by paying attention to national context of tenure wages and employment protection (ordered logistic regression analysis)

	Denmark		France		Germany		Italy	
	Explaining labour cost-productivity gap by paying attention to country specific effects of [a]							
	Odds ratio	Z-value	Odds ratio	Z-value	Odds ratio	Z-value	Odds ratio	Z-value
Main effects								
Tenure wage	1.17**	3.63	1.20**	4.54	1.13**	2.85	1.19**	4.15
Employment protection	1.11*	2.54	1.12**	3.12	1.10*	2.38	1.13**	3.22
Two way interactions								
Tenure wage *Country	1.10	0.87	0.82	-1.50	1.29*	2.39	0.95	-0.46
Employment protection *Country	1.12	1.31	1.05	0.41	1.24*	2.10	0.98	-0.26
Control variables	Yes		Yes		Yes		Yes	
Pseudo R^2	0.08		0.08		0.08		0.08	
N	4,947		4,947		4,947		4,947	

	Explaining labour cost-productivity gap by paying attention to country specific effects of[a]					
	Netherlands		Poland		Sweden	
	Odds ratio	z-value	Odds ratio	z-value	Odds ratio	z-value
Main effects						
Tenure wage	1.15**	3.49	1.22**	4.62	1.21**	4.55
Employment protection	1.13**	3.32	1.14**	3.35	1.18**	4.27
Two way interactions						
Tenure wage *Country	1.31*	2.02	0.85	-1.80	0.86	-1.26
Employment protection *Country	0.97	-0.23	0.94	-0.65	0.75**	-2.86
Control variables[b]	Yes		Yes		Yes	
Pseudo R^2	0.08		0.08		0.08	
N	4,947		4,947		4,947	

*Significant at $p < .05$; ** significant at $p < .01$.

Notes: [a] Dependent variable: labour cost-productivity gap, country name: country in two-way interaction terms.
[b] Controlled for: sector of industry, organisational features (size, share of high-skilled workers, share of workers with fixed-term temporary contract, share of older workers, extent of absenteeism/sickness rate), countries.

Source: ASPA Employers Survey (2009).

List of NIDI books/reports

88. Wieteke Conen, *Older workers: The view of Dutch employers in a European perspective*, 2013, pp. 162.

87. Kène Henkens, Harry van Dalen en Hanna van Solinge, *Doorwerken over de drempel van het pensioen (Working beyond retirement)*, 2013, pp. 124.

86. Nico van Nimwegen en Carlo van Praag (red.), *Bevolkingsvraagstukken in Nederland anno 2012: actief ouder worden in Nederland (Population issues in the Netherlands, 2012: active ageing in the Netherlands)*, Werkverband Periodieke Rapportage Bevolkingsvraagstukken, 2012, pp. 195.

85. Harry van Dalen, Kène Henkens, Wieteke Conen en Joop Schippers, *Dilemma's rond langer doorwerken: Europese werkgevers aan het woord. (Dilemmas in active ageing: What do European employers say)*, 2012, pp. 128.

84. Marcel Ham en Jelle van der Meer, *De etnische bril: Categorisering in het integratiebeleid*, 2012, pp. 72.

83. Joop de Beer, *Transparency in population forecasting: Methods for fitting and projecting fertility, mortality and migration.* 2011, pp. 256.

82. Nico van Nimwegen, *Demography Monitor 2008. Demographic trends, socio-economic impacts and policy implications in the European Union*, 2010, pp. 161.

81. Judith P.M. Soons, *Love, life and happiness: A study of partner relationships and well-being in young adulthood*, 2009, pp. 175.

80. Nico van Nimwegen en Liesbeth Heering, *Bevolkingsvraagstukken in Nederland anno 2009: Van groei naar krinp. Een demografische omslag in beeld. (Population issues in the Netherlands, 2009: From population growth to decline. Perspectives on a demographic turning point)*, 2009, pp. 240.

79. Anne Elisabeth van Putten, *The role of intergenerational transfers in gendered labour patterns*, 2009, pp. 215.

78. Kène Henkens, Harry van Dalen en Hanna van Solinge, *De vervagende grens tussen werk en pensioen: over doorwerkers, doorstarters en herintreders. (The fading line between work and pension)*, 2009, pp. 129.

77. Pearl A. Dykstra, *Ageing, intergenerational solidarity and age-specific vulnerabilities*, 2008, pp. 167.

76. Tineke Fokkema, Susan ter Bekke en Pearl A. Dykstra, *Solidarity between parents and their adult children in Europe*, 2008. pp. 125.

75. Harry van Dalen en Kène Henkens, *Weg uit Nederland: emigratie aan het begin van de 21ᵉ eeuw, (Leaving the Netherlands: Emigration at the start of the 21ˢᵗ century)*, 2008, pp. 134.

74. Harry van Dalen, Kène Henkens en Joop Schippers, *Oudere werknemers door de lens van de werkgever, (Older employees through the eyes of the employer)*, 2007, pp. 122. € 11,50.

A NIDI report (1-74) can be ordered by remitting the amount due, plus postage and administrative costs (€ 5,00), to bank account number 45.83.68.687 (ABN-AMRO, The Hague) in the name of NIDI-KNAW, The Hague, mentioning the relevant report number with reference to the SWIFT-code: ABNANL2A and the IBAN-code: NL56ABNA0458368687. The address of the ABN-AMRO is P.O. BOX 90, 1000 AB in Amsterdam. If you wish to order more than one report, please telephone us (+31-70-3565200) as the editions are limited.

Report 75 et cetera can be ordered at Amsterdam University Press, Herengracht 221, 1016 BG Amsterdam, info@aup.nl, www.aup.nl

(Subject to changes)

For Product Safety Concerns and Information please contact our EU
representative GPSR@taylorandfrancis.com
Taylor & Francis Verlag GmbH, Kaufingerstraße 24, 80331 München, Germany